P9-DMS-827

The Gardener's Gripe Book

The Gardener's Gripe Book

**MUSINGS, ADVICE AND COMFORT
FOR ANYONE WHO HAS EVER
SUFFERED THE LOSS OF A PETUNIA**

BY ABBY ADAMS
ILLUSTRATED BY JEFF SEAVER

Workman Publishing, New York

Text copyright © 1995 by Abby Adams.
Art copyright © 1995 by Jeff Seaver.

All rights reserved. No portion of this book may be reproduced—
mechanically, electronically, or by any other means, including photo-
copying—without written permission of the publisher. Published
simultaneously in Canada by Thomas Allen & Son Limited.

Library of Congress Cataloging-in-Publication Data
    Adams, Abby.
        The gardener's gripe book : musings, advice and comfort for anyone
    who has ever suffered the loss of a petunia / by Abby Adams.
            p.   cm.
        ISBN 1-56305-647-X (paper)
        1. Gardening—Miscellanea.   2. Gardening—Humor.   I. Title.
    SB455.A43   1995
    635'.0207—dc20   94-44834
                                                                CIP4

Excerpts:
From *Gardening with Groundcovers and Vines* by Allen Lacy and Cynthia
    Woodyard. Text copyright © 1993 by Allen Lacy. Illustrations
    copyright © 1993 by Cynthia Woodyard. Reprinted by permission
    of HarperCollins Publishers, Inc.
From *Garden Smarts*. Copyright © 1991 by Shelley Goldbloom.
    Reprinted by permission of Globe Pequot Press, Old Saybrook, CT.
From *Green Thoughts* by Eleanor Perenyi. Copyright© 1981 by
    Eleanor Perenyi. Reprinted by permission of Random House, Inc.
From *The New York Times*. Copyright © 1992/93/94/95 by The New
    York Times Company. Reprinted by permission.
From *The Practical Gardener* by Roger Swain. Copyright © 1989 by
    Roger B. Swain. By permission of Little, Brown and Company.
From *Second Nature* by Michael Pollan. Copyright © 1991 by Michael
    Pollan. Reprinted by permission of Grove/Atlantic, Inc.

Workman books are available at special discounts when purchased in
bulk for premiums and sales promotions as well as for fundraising or
educational use. Special editions or book excerpts can also be created
to specification. For details, please contact the Special Sales Director
at the address below.

Workman Publishing
708 Broadway
New York, NY 10003-9555
www.workman.com

Manufactured in the United States of America

10 9 8 7 6 5 4 3 2

This book is dedicated to my grandparents, Charles Cyrus Washburn (1862–1944) and Myrtie Harlow Washburn (1866–1959). They were farmers. As I slog about the garden, I often find myself wondering what they would make of my efforts. Would they be amused? Impressed? Scornful? This book is for them, wherever they may be, to make of what they will.

I also dedicate this book to my husband, Donald Westlake, whose job it was to call me in out of the garden from time to time so that I could write it.

CONTENTS

The Gardener's Gripe Book

INTRODUCTION

Awhile ago I told a friend of mine, who happens to be a landscape designer, that I was writing a gardening book. My friend gazed down his nose at me, and said: *"You?"* Meaning: "You! rank amateur that you are; what can you possibly have to say about gardening?" Were David American (he's a Brit), he might have said: "Where do you get off?"

This is where I get off: I grew up in a dark, grimy apartment in Greenwich Village, in New York City. My mother, who had been raised on a farm in Maine, always missed the country, though she had a horror of small-town life. I remember forlorn little philodendrons that quickly died because, in fact, my mother had a very black thumb. (It isn't easy to kill a philodendron.) In March she would buy wooden boxes of chives from the Italian pushcart vendors on Bleecker Street, and for a few days the impossibly green blades would bring life into our kitchen. And then, long before the trees outside leafed out, the chives would turn yellow and wither and die; a little bit of memento mori right there on our kitchen window.

A few years ago, reading Eleanor Perenyi's terrific book *Green*

THE GARDENER'S GRIPE BOOK

Thoughts, I learned that my mother's chives were heir to an ancient tradition of "Adonis gardens": pots or baskets that women planted with quick-growing seed to herald the return of spring and re-birth of the god. It's just as well my mother didn't try to follow this tradition literally, because any seed she tried to grow invariably didn't.

The first garden I ever made was sort of an Adonis basket; it was a miniature landscape in a glass bowl, with moss trees and pebble mountains, and a tiny bridge over a pocket-mirror lake. It was a school project. I entered it in the Macy's Flower Show, where it did not capture any prizes. But I thought it was wonderful. I can still smell its sweet, rich, peaty aroma, the essence of spring.

In the years since then I've had a lot of different gardens here and there, small and large: from a few pots on a back porch in San Francisco, to a vegetable garden deep in the woods in Woodstock, New York; from a run-down farm in western New Jersey, to a window box in Knightsbridge, London. For almost twenty years I divided my gardening efforts between a terrace in New York City and a sandy, deer-infested plot of land on Fire Island. But it was not until a few years ago, when my husband and I bought a ten-acre former farm in upstate New York, deep in the wilds of zone 5, that I became a Gardener.

I remember that first summer: I would spend the days humping wheelbarrow loads of plants and dirt and stones around the property; then in the evenings I would sit, with graph paper and ruler, and make Plans; then finally, at bedtime, I'd drag my tired, aching body upstairs, only to spend another hour or two with the towering stack of garden books and catalogs and magazines beside the bed. And when I finally did get to sleep I'd dream of gardens: beautiful, trouble-free gardens, like the ones in the pictures.

Every morning was a rude awakening as the green lawns of my fantasies were replaced by the hard, sere surface outside the door; the cascading roses and towering delphiniums turned into a few flowers and a lot of weeds.

In an effort to close the gap between dreams and reality I joined horticultural societies, took courses, attended lectures. When, rarely, I would tear myself away from the country and go to New York—or London or Paris—I'd invariably wind up in parks and flower shows and botanical gardens and farmers' markets. I was truly hooked.

And I wasn't alone. Gardening, as recently reported in *The New York Times*, had become the nation's "No. 1 hobby." Folks were buying peonies on the QVC shopping network. Membership in garden clubs was soaring. When Martha Stewart went on television to praise hydrangeas, they sold out in nurseries coast to coast. All of which is really weird considering that, as only a casual glance around can tell you, most people don't have gardens at all. And when they do, they don't look even remotely like the ones in the glossy pictures.

Meanwhile my own garden was bumping along, with dazzling successes, tragic failures, and lots of brutally hard work in between. Mysterious blights and vengeful predators proved much harder to cope with than any of the garden literature had suggested. It wasn't that there was a shortage of answers to my problems; there was a veritable glut of answers, many of which were contradictory, silly, or simply false. Some of the experts, I came to realize, didn't actually know that much; some of them told *lies.*

Even when the answers were clear-cut, following all the directions didn't guarantee success. I learned that plants have a will of their own, and sometimes it is a will to die.

All the while, money was hemorrhaging out of our pockets. We needed so much stuff! We made almost daily runs to the local hardware store to stock up on gardening gadgets and tools and nostrums. Huge bags of peat moss and grass seed, a wheelbarrow to transport them, then a pickup truck so we could go to the garden center for another load of "plant material." Each day's mail brought more occasions for spending. How about some kidskin work gloves? A forged-steel manure fork? A few million beneficial bugs? Labor was the most expensive luxury of all— worth almost every penny when we could get it, which wasn't often . . .

Without ever slackening in my passion for gardening I found myself assembling a list of quibbles and peeves and gripes, which in time became this book.

This book differs from other garden books in several ways:

I AM NOT AN EXPERT. I barely know enough to keep my own garden going, nowhere near enough to tell anyone else what to do. I'm learning all the time, and then unlearning what I just learned. If you shook my brain, half-digested bits of garden wisdom would fall out: words like *chelated*, and *thalictrum*, and *half-hardy*, and *nematode*, and *double digging*, and *diatomaceous*, and *fish emulsion*, and *striated*; along with flowers and seeds and half a pair of muddy gloves, and a tangle of twist ties, and a plant label, perhaps for that delphinium that didn't make it.

I DO NOT HAVE A GREEN THUMB. On Fire Island we had a neighbor who had a green thumb; in the spring when he pruned his roses, he stuck the prunings in the sandy soil and each year more than half of them took root and made new rosebushes. When I tried to do this, more than ninety percent died. In fact, they all died. (I didn't inherit my mother's black thumb. Mine is sort of skin-colored; although sometimes when I'm feeding Peters to the house-plants it turns blue-green.)

Admitting to yourself that you do not have a green thumb is very liberating; I recommend it. In fact, the more you recognize that the plants are actually doing the work and you are just there to watch and occasionally save them from disaster (anyone who has ever taught a child to ride a bicycle will know how to do this), the better for everyone.

I AM NOT A CHEERLEADER. This is not another "Joy of Gardening." I love to garden, but I do not think anything about it is easy or simple or even natural.

This book is for people like me who find gardening a fascinating and maddening and frustrating and absorbing endeavor. It will bring solace to those who have suffered the sad and often inexplicable loss of a beloved plant companion. I promise not to wax lyrical or mystical, or to offer glib, easy solutions to difficult problems like the spreading crud on the roses. I will tell no lies.

WHAT IS A GARDEN, ANYWAY?

Confusion about gardening begins with the word itself. According to Webster's, a garden is "land for the cultivation of flowers, vegetables, or fruit." In the *Oxford English Dictionary* it's "an enclosed piece of ground devoted to the cultivation of flowers, fruit, or vegetables." (That distinction—between "land" and "an enclosed piece of ground"—points out just one of the many ways in which American gardens differ from their British forebears.)

Neither definition allows for gardens of trees or shrubs, or for non-plant gardens: Japanese gardens of gravel and rock; formal European parterres in which colored sand, crushed glass and even coal dust take the place of living plants. Neither one accounts for gardens not on land or ground, like those in conservatories, or that array of dusty philodendrons and palms on yonder windowsill.

There are places that are called gardens, but aren't. When my friend Gloria Scott, who is a landscape designer, visited Toronto she spotted something on the map that appealed to her; it was called Maple Leaf Gardens. She and her husband put on their walking shoes and made their way to it, to find—a baseball stadium.

A stadium is not a garden. Neither is an arena like Madison

Square Garden. We can also exclude market gardens and garden centers and pleasure gardens, along with the Garden Of Allah and the Garden State.

A state—even if it's New Jersey—cannot be a garden. Gardens are *limited.* They may be as small as a tiny landscape in a dish, or as big as Versailles, but they can't be as big as all outdoors; that is nature.

A garden is not nature. We speak of wildflower gardening and naturalistic gardening, and harnessing or working in partnership with nature, but the fact of the matter is, nature and the gardener have different goals. Nature is what knocks the hollyhocks over in a thunderstorm; hatches a zillion voracious cabbage worms; sends rhizomes of crabgrass creeping through the sod, heading toward the flower border. Nature is what takes over when the gardener turns his or her back.

A garden isn't a farm, either. A farm, to quote Webster's again, is "land cultivated for agricultural purposes." Agriculture—a big clunky serious word. Agriculture isn't fun, and although it's sometimes hard to keep in mind—in April, for instance, when your boots are filling up with mud and icy rain is sliding down the back of your neck as you labor to replace the rocks in your garden with living plants—gardening is supposed to be a *pleasure.*

There are as many kinds of gardens as there are gardeners, and they define themselves across sharp aesthetic and philosophical lines: utility versus beauty; vegetables versus ornamentals; chemicals versus organics; formal style versus naturalistic. Different countries breed different gardeners.

In America, when people ask "Do you have a garden?" they

usually aren't thinking of perennials, or roses, or azaleas, and they certainly aren't thinking of expanses of raked sand; they're thinking of tomatoes and lettuces, neatly lined up in rows.

In England they're more likely to mean flowers and ornamentals. Gardening in England is a hobby, about midway on the social scale between throwing darts and composing sonnets. Even the growing of vegetables has been turned into a sport, a quest for record-breaking fruit—twenty-pound tomatoes, half-ton marrows, three-foot-long carrots.

"Gardening is a luxury occupation," writes Vita Sackville-West; and the practitioner "one of the few people left in this distressful world to carry on the tradition of elegance and charm." In our heart of hearts, we American gardeners may think of ourselves as artists, but we'd rather eat out of the compost heap than admit it. We're much more comfortable growing organic melons, or striking a blow for ethnobotanical diversity, than we are with Beauty.

We are also uneasy with the notion that as gardeners we are working *against* nature.

Gardeners are—let's face it—control freaks. Who else would willingly spend his leisure hours wresting weeds out of the ground, blithely making life or death decisions about living beings, moving earth from here to there, changing the course of waterways? The more one thinks about it, the odder it seems; this compulsion to remake a little corner of the planet according to some plan or vision.

Some people are made very uncomfortable by the realization that as gardeners we are playing God. These are the people who plant butterfly gardens and grow wildflowers and find beauty and

even nutrition in their weeds. These are the people who rip up their lawns to grow native trees. But the very act of planting and growing and ripping up puts us at odds with nature. A garden is not nature. Isn't it better to acknowledge this and accept the responsibility than to try to duck it by pretending that one is Mother Nature's handmaiden (or handyman)? There's not really that much difference between an ecologically correct meadow and the manicured, not-a-petal-out-of-place flower beds that surround the war memorial in the village green.

A garden, then, is a finite place, in which a gardener (or several gardeners) has created, working with or against nature, a plot whose intention it is to provide pleasure; possibly in the form of beauty, possibly in the form of cabbages—and possibly, beautiful cabbages.

And nature? Nature is what wins in the end.

EVERYTHING I KNOW ABOUT GARDENING I LEARNED FROM MY HOUSEPLANTS

THE MICROCOSM

About twenty years ago—from the late 1960s to the mid-'70s—there was a craze for houseplants. In New York City, plant stores sprang up like mushrooms after a rain. There were books about houseplants, newspaper columns about houseplants, even a PBS television series with Thalassa Cruso doing for dracaenas what Julia Child was doing for duxelles.

People bought avocados to turn into houseplants, and someone even wrote a book about avocado-growing; and other people—including me—*bought* it. A book suggesting that plants could and should be talked to hit the best-seller list. At cocktail parties folks discussed their ailing podocarpus, the way nowadays they talk about their roses. A friend of mine launched a successful business in New York City, watering and grooming houseplants in apartments while the owners were away. (She hired underemployed actors and called it "Rain Dears.")

But eventually, like all fads, the houseplant craze expired, leaving behind a few dusty, fading palms. The plant stores became video parlors. My friend became a caterer.

I well remember the first houseplant I ever bought; it was (and

11

still is) an asparagus fern. I bought it in, I think, 1966, at a store at the corner of Perry Street and Bleecker, and its wrought-iron plant stand—originally black, then white, now green—at the same store, in 1980 at their going-out-of-business sale.

There were a lot of other plants between then and now, and some that died. I still feel bad about the creeping fig—ugly name for such a dainty little vine—although I wasn't too sorry when those ungainly avocado trees met their demise.

I fretted over my poor tropical plants, struggling for survival in a dark, dry city apartment. I watched Thalassa Cruso, I listened to Stan and Floss. I watered my plants, I misted them, I fed them; I even tried talking to them.

My plants' lower leaves turned yellow and I turned to the books. I learned that yellowing lower leaves could be caused by underwatering. Or overwatering. Or not enough light, or inadequate humidity, or being "potbound," or some nasty disease. It was my first experience with garden books and should have warned me.

One book suggested discarding plants after a couple of years and replacing them; perhaps the author was in the pay of that shop on Perry Street. Another book told me to

"In Russia, millions of newspaper readers were introduced to the idea that plants communicate their feelings to man in October, 1970, when Pravda *published an article entitled 'What Leaves Tell Us.'*

'Plants talk . . . yes, they scream,' declared the official organ of the Communist party. 'It only seems that they accept their misfortunes submissively.'"

Peter Tompkins and
Christopher Bird
The Secret Life
of Plants

repot my plants every year, but the instructions were so complicated, and the whole procedure seemed so perilous, that I wound up leaving the plants in their old pots, year after year.

Time passed, the way it does, and I lost interest in my houseplants. I wouldn't say I stopped liking them, but I no longer included them in my prayers, and when I did speak to them I spoke less sweetly. My sister-in-law claims she once heard me say, to an especially scraggly palm, "If I stop watering you, will you die, please?"

I still have the asparagus fern and almost every other houseplant I've ever owned, with their offspring, and I still have all those books although it's been years since I consulted them. The plants live a miserable light-deprived, potbound, low-humidity life for seven months of the year. Then, on the first nice day in May, they go outside to the terrace for the summer. Even though all those books I used to read cautioned never to let houseplants out of doors, they thrive, like city children at a Fresh Air Camp. Actually my terrace, between the beating rains and the baking droughts, and the occasional squirrel attack, is more like an Outward Bound. But the

". . . I have always disliked houseplants. I would hate to see any of them go, however. They are like a rabbit that you wish you didn't have (we had a vicious one for years and years) but that you get used to feeding and watering every day forever and therefore miss when it dies at twice the usual age of rabbits. And these plants are much like the Vietnam War—once you have invested enough labor and woe, you are strangely unwilling to acknowledge that it was a stupid mistake to begin with. You just go on and on."

Henry Mitchell
One Man's Garden

plants love it out there. They change color, from olive drab to glossy green. They send out new shoots and even flowers, and the more fecund of them divide and multiply. I imagine that during the long winters they dream of their summer vacations, and the hope keeps them alive.

THE MACROCOSM

A few years ago my husband and I bought a house in the country. As a gardener I felt as if I'd moved into the major leagues; our new ten-plus acres made the city terrace look like a terrarium. Coincidentally, this occurred at almost exactly the moment in history when gardening became America's favorite pastime; I was part of the Zeitgeist.

Suddenly there was so much to learn: about botany and climate and design and wildlife, and why the dogwood leaves had spots on them; and whether to plant holly or andromeda or laurel behind the house; and when was it safe to move the tomato plants outside. The stakes were higher now—much higher; that ailing dogwood, should it be replaced, could cost as much as several *hundred* creeping figs.

I immersed myself in garden literature, greedily devouring information from every source I could find. And the more I learned, the more confused I became.

The experts disagreed with each other and even with themselves. No sooner had I learned how to plant a tree—dig a deep hole, mix in a lot of peat moss and fertilizer, prune, water thoroughly—than along came a new method: dig a *wide* hole, *don't* use peat moss or fertilizer, and whatever you do, *don't prune.* Next they'd be telling me not to water. I wanted to get it right, but what was right?

It brought back memories of those puzzling yellow leaves, and the drooping avocado plants. Would there ever come a time, I wondered, when my trees and rosebushes and perennials would become comfortable familiars like that old asparagus fern?

I thought about my twenty years of houseplant mothering—I must have learned a few things along the way. Was there any way I could put that experience to use in the great out-of-doors? After all, plants are plants, and what works indoors ought to apply outside too.

It turned out that there are a few general principles I've learned over the years, learned the hard way through pain and suffering—not all of it the plants'.

GROOMING. What you do about those yellow leaves on your houseplants is, I eventually realized, pluck them off. Most of the time the plant won't grow any others. If it does, pluck them off, too. This advice holds for all plants, big and small, inside and out. It's one of the advantages plants have over

us; they can lose leaves and even big limbs and then grow new ones.

It always amazes me how people can puzzle and puzzle over a yellow leaf or dead branch, and fail to get rid of it. Some people even like to keep dead trees around while they wonder about what killed them. Pluck it out! And get the horrid thing off the property in case what it's got is catching.

THOROUGH WATERING. One of the surest ways to kill a houseplant, I've learned, is to tease it with little splashes of water. This is equivalent to giving your garden a quick spritz with the hose every night, during a drought. Never mind that this is fun for the gardener; it's bad for the garden. The plants send out lots of feeble little surface roots, which creep around in a hopeless search for water. Meanwhile the real roots aren't getting anything and they atrophy, and by and by the whole plant dies. Most plants—and this is true of trees and bushes and even lawn grass—like a good soaking, with drier periods in between.

The other crime is to overwater your plant so that it sits for days in a saucer of stale water. The roots suffocate. You can achieve the same deadly effect out of doors by planting things in an area with very poor drainage, like that mossy spot at the bottom of the lawn where water stands after a rain. Which brings me to

LOCATION. Location location location, as they say in real estate. Light, I learned, is more important to houseplants—and all plants—even than water. The reason the poor little creeping fig expired was that I put it in a dark room, then compounded the offense by closing the curtains. In four days it was dead. Just as well, otherwise it might have lived a long, miserable and ugly life. Creeping fig wants to be a ground cover outside in Southern California, not a pot plant in a New York apartment.

Every gardener has had the sad experience of plants that simply won't accept a certain environment. No matter that you dream of having clematis vines festooned along the balustrade, turning the porch into a bower of purple blossoms; the clematis hates it there. With houseplants, of course, you can simply pick them up and move them, but it's not all *that* difficult with larger plants, once you develop

AUTHORITY. You gotta make it clear that you're the boss. Plants can't drive to the Agway and buy fertilizer; they can't pinch off their suckers or prune their roots or zap their parasites; for all this they need you, and they should be damn grateful. As with children, a firm touch is appreciated. And as with children (I can hear my own guffawing at this), it's not that easily achieved.

My houseplants have learned to acknowledge my authority; they know that when I tell them they don't need fertilizer, no matter what the books say, I'm right. The dumb cane (a.k.a. dieffenbachia) knows that when I chop off his three-foot-tall cane to make a new, shorter plant, it's for his own good.

In the country garden my mastery is yet to

". . . I took a quick look at the windowsill, where the geraniums, with hardly a leaf or flower to bless themselves with, were tangled in an imploring mass against the dusty panes like debtors at a grating in the Fleet Prison. Each of their pots was a Sahara in miniature where the Red spiders scuttled precariously between the tiny chasms in the dried-up earth. . . . I was peering through these skeletal geraniums when Miss Murry returned. 'They want watering,' I told her indignantly. 'I daresay they do,' she said. 'But if we all got what we wanted we'd be marchionesses, wouldn't we?'"

Ronald Blythe,
in A Book of Gardens

be fully acknowledged. I doubt the old maples will ever accept me, and the dogwood may prefer death. I suspect the rosebushes of making rude comments behind my back. But I do like to think I'm making headway with the perennials; they no longer cringe when they see me coming, trowel in hand, but sit up expectantly waiting for the next adventure.

FOLLOW SUCCESS. Yes, we learn from our failures, but we learn more from our successes. The thing to do with a failure is to accept it, and move on; endlessly trying to figure out what went wrong will only bring you down, like worrying about why people don't like you. You may never know why the ficus died! You could buy another ficus, or you could look around the living room and see what's thriving—perhaps an asparagus fern—and learn to enjoy its graceful fronds and jaunty red berries in winter.

Here in my country garden the big success story is the tulips. Contrary to all my previous experience, these tulips grow like gangbusters. Not only do they come up reliably every year, flowering when and in the colors promised in the catalogs; they actually *increase* in number from year to year. The moles and squirrels and deer seem to leave them alone.

"We don't put our houseplants outside for spring and summer. . . . It just leads to trauma, leaf loss, and bug problems when we come to bring them inside in the fall."

Floss and Stan Dworkin
Floss & Stan's "Why are my leaves turning yellow and falling off?" Answer Book

Now, I can't really take any credit for all this because there were tulips growing happily on the property when we bought it. As all the literature insists that tulips are so shortlived it's better to dig them up each year than to expect return bloom, I'm a bit baffled by my success. I'm baffled by the literature, too; you can understand why a bulb catalog would advise you to buy new tulip bulbs each year, but why do all the garden books go along with it? It's a good thing I didn't follow their counsel.

Since then I've added a lot of bulbs—lilies and daffs and crocus and their ilk, and many more tulips, and they've all done well, too, knock on wood. They are a great consolation to me when the tree hydrangea refuses to flower, the dogwood languishes, and the roses . . . Never mind the roses. I will know that I've achieved true wisdom when I stop trying to grow roses.

USE WHAT YOU HAVE. That same terrace in the city contains, besides the houseplants, several large tubs that must be filled with "plant material" every summer. (One of the tubs is, in fact, a cast-iron claw-footed bathtub with a crab apple tree sort of growing in it.) I used to go out and spend a lot of money buying flats of plants to fill the tubs, until I hit on the idea of pulling off the little spider babies from the spider plants and sticking them in the soil. They fill out very quickly and, by autumn, are producing babies themselves. I've had similar success with Swedish ivy

cuttings. As the Swedish ivy was received as a gift in 1974, and the spiders are all descendants of one little spiderlet pinched from a plant growing in a bar window on West Fourth Street in 1981, these are major economies, to my mind, and entitle me to go to the garden center and buy tray upon tray of begonias.

I learned to do similar tricks in the country, although I'm more likely to divide or dig up a whole plant than to chop off a branch and expect it to take hold.

It began with the spireas. There were lots of them: big, ungainly shrubs that looked heavenly for two weeks in May, briefly justifying their common name, Bridal Wreath. Soon after we bought the place we rerouted the driveway and had to move several spireas. We dug them up (I use the pronoun "we" in this case to indicate that I told somebody else what to do), not sure whether they'd made it, but with the attitude that if they didn't it wouldn't be a great loss. The spireas were so unflustered by the experience that they bloomed on schedule a few weeks later. When we needed shrubs to stick in front of the pool fence, we re-dug up some of these, and then, a year or

" 'O Tiger-lily!' said Alice, addressing herself to one that was waving gracefully about in the wind, 'I wish you could talk!'

'We can talk,' said the Tiger-lily, 'when there's anybody worth talking to.'"

Lewis Carroll
Alice's Adventures in Wonderland

so later, the fence had to be moved and the spireas moved with it. (Someone—a digging someone—suggested we replace their roots with wheels.)

It came as a revelation that, with all their peregrinations, the ambulatory spireas were growing as well as or better than their stick-in-the-mud cousins. I began moving other plants around. Three coralbells *(Heuchera)* in the perennial border came up easily and just as easily divided into nine plants, which soon became twenty, then a border on their own, as inexhaustible a resource as the spider plants. And if some plants didn't exactly thrive under this treatment, I always had spireas and coralbells to fill in the gaps.

Now, if I could just learn to be content with a landscape of nothing but spireas and coralbells, with maybe a few tulips in the spring, I'd be a happy person.

COMMUNICATION. I still talk to plants, indoors and out, though I've given up trying to educate them. I say things like "Aren't you pretty!" and "Oh you sweet thing" when I'm pleased. At other times I might say, "Bloom, damn you," or "If you don't behave, I'm going to put you out on the sidewalk."

Communication goes both ways, of course. These are some of the things plants say: "There are ten million aphids on my buds and they itch." "Those hideous magenta phlox are hogging all the water." "I want to go back to the garden center."

The truest lessons my houseplants have taught me are the ones I refuse to learn.

First, to trust my own judgment and stop reading those confusing books. But I'm as addicted to reading about gardens as I am to gardening.

Second, and most important, to keep the garden small and manageable—like a collection of potted plants on a terrace.

I can't do it. Having made the leap from microcosm to macrocosm, I'm doomed to keep on expanding, year after year—adding a bed of *fraises des bois* to the vegetable plot; a yellow-orange flower border beside the pool fence; a pumpkin and sunflower garden up on the hill; a wildflower collection under the trees to the west of the house . . . There is no turning back.

FROM EVE TO MARTHA STEWART

A Brief History of Gardening

It began so well. The attractive young couple, Adam and Eve, cloaked in their innocence and nothing else; set up by a generous father in a beautiful garden with "every tree that is pleasant to the sight and good for food." No mention of weeds or powdery mildew. Beasts of the field and fowl of the air so tame they answer to their names. Four rivers that not only bring water to the garden, but lead to lands rich in gold and onyx. The young couple's only task is to "dress and keep" the garden. And by the by, don't eat any fruit from that big tree in the middle.

And then it all went to hell.

Ever since then, people have argued over whom to blame. Poor Eve is usually thought the culprit. I myself blame Dad; I think he made the rules too tough. If you've nothing to do all day except sit around in some garden and *not* eat apples, sooner or later you *will*. (Of course, they weren't really apples; apples didn't come along until eons and eons later.)

The Garden of Eden was in the Middle East, somewhere in what is now Iraq and was then Mesopotamia. One of those four rivers was the Euphrates, which, together with the Tigris, bordered

"And the Lord God planted a garden eastward in Eden; and there he put the man whom he had formed. And out of the ground made the Lord God to grow every tree that is pleasant to the sight, and good for food; the tree of life also in the midst of the garden, and the tree of knowledge of good and evil. . . . And the Lord God commanded the man, saying, Of every tree of the garden thou mayest freely eat: But of the tree of knowledge of good and evil, thou shalt not eat of it. . . ."

the Book of Genesis,
Chapter 2

the famed Fertile Crescent. Originally this crescent was mostly swamp, home to an early form of the pestiferous reed grass *Phragmites australis.* Some seven thousand years ago, the early Sumerians drained the marshes and constructed canals, turning this unpromising area into the cradle of Western civilization. (Having battled phragmites myself, I take my hat off to the Sumerians.)

Nowadays the entire Arabian Peninsula is barren desert—which is what comes of draining wetlands to create civilizations and gardens—but even in biblical times the Middle East was pretty arid. Gardens then and now were walled oases in the desert, verdant refuges from the hostile climate. Plantings were laid out in neat geometric rows, surrounding elaborate water features such as fountains, canals and fish ponds.

Were there gardens in prehistory? Did the cavemen and cavewomen garden? Did Mrs. Flintstone tuck a few ur-petunias into the clay outside her cave? We'll never know.

Garden history has little to say about such humble efforts, in any era. It is also mostly mute on the nuts-and-bolts side of horticulture; on matters such as slugs, rainfall or the lack thereof, rampant weeds, inhospitable soil, nongerminating seeds—all the issues that we gardeners fret over. And as real gardens seldom last long, rarely surviving more than a couple of seasons of neglect, archaeological traces are scant. Most of what we know of past gardens comes from pictures and written records, which celebrate an ideal rather than the reality; it's as though a future civilization were to learn about our horticultural attempts from the pages of the White Flower Farm catalog.

". . . that I may each day walk continuously on the banks of my water, that my soul may repose on the branches of the trees that I have planted, that I may refresh myself under the shade of my sycamore."

standard inscription in Egyptian tombs of the New Kingdom

ANCIENT EDENS

Given the Egyptian practice of entombing everything, their gardening efforts are well documented. One of the very earliest records comes from a tomb dated about 2000 B.C., a dollhouse-size wooden replica of a walled garden, with a fish pond and fig trees.

Even in those long-ago times, gardeners were a discontented breed, always on the lookout for the rare or unusual. In the Eighteenth Dynasty (c. 1470 B.C.) Queen Hatshepsut, "for whom all Egypt was made to labor with bowed head," imported thirty-one frankincense trees, their roots balled up in baskets, from Somalia. They did not survive, making Hatshepsut one of garden history's earliest brown thumbs.

"From outside the court, by its entry, extends a great garden of four acres, fenced each way. In it flourish tall trees: pears or pomegranates, stone fruits gaudy with their ripening load, also sweet figs and heavy bearing olives. The fruit of these trees never blights or fails to set, winter and summer, through all the years. A west wind blows there perpetually, maturing one crop and making another. . . . Vegetable beds are neatly laid out and make a smiling patch of never-failing green. The garden is served by two springs. . . ."

Homer,
"Alcinous' Garden"
The Odyssey

The ancient Persians are responsible for the notion of the garden as a model of heaven. Like the Garden of Eden, their private paradises (the word "paradise" comes from a Persian word for "garden") contained flowers, lush fruit trees, running water (often in four canals intersecting in the center, like the rivers in Eden) and cool shade.

History's very first example of the garden as an exercise in conspicuous consumption was the Hanging Gardens of Babylon. This extravaganza was built by King Nebuchadnezzar II (605–562 B.C.) to please his wife Amytis, a Persian girl who pined for the mountains of home. The gardens covered some three acres of aboveground terraces in the middle of downtown Babylon. Hollow pillars filled with soil supported tall trees, and water was brought from the Euphrates by means of a sophisticated hydraulic system. Their fame was such that they were known as one of the Seven Wonders of the World, as famous in their day as Versailles was later on. Did Queen Amytis enjoy the Hanging Gardens, and her position as garden style-setter of the ancient world, or did she continue to yearn for her peaceful childhood Eden? Alas, Amytis left no diary.

During the Roman Empire, private gardens evolved from the simple enclosures of the Persians and the Egyptians into elaborate and extensive constructs. Graceful outdoor living is not a California invention—it is Roman. Accomplished engineers, the Romans created intricate water systems: fountains, cascades, aqueducts, spas. They invented the heated swimming pool. They were plant collectors, acquiring specimens from the countries they conquered and planting their favorites—roses, lilies, herbs, grapes for wine, olives, fruit trees—wherever they went.

The Romans were the first to clip their hedges, often into fanciful shapes. Topiary is a Roman invention: in Latin the word *topiarius* means "gardener." Wealthy Romans paid their gardeners well and vied for their services.

"Your gardener has so enveloped everything with ivy, not only the foundation walls of the villa, but also the spaces between the columns of the promenade, that I declare the Greek statues seem to be in business as landscape designers, and to be advertising ivy."

Cicero, in a letter to his brother Quintus, 54 B.C.

27

"Within the grounds Hui Yuan laid out a grove for meditation. The mist condensed on the trees and dripped on the mossy paths. Every spot seen by the eye and trodden by the foot was full of spiritual purity and majesty."

description of a monastery, fourth-century manuscript

MEANWHILE

On the other side of the world a very different tradition had begun. The Chinese landscape, with its lush diversity of vegetation and its dramatic mountains and chasms, inspired a more irregular, naturalistic style.

Chinese gardening dates back to about 2000 B.C. and the legendary Emperor Wu's wish to re-create the mythical Chinese eden, believed to lie somewhere in the Mystic Isles in the North China Sea. With paths and bridges and craggy rocks, Chinese gardeners created fantastic dream landscapes, in which the various elements were valued as much for their symbolic meaning as for their beauty.

Around 600 B.C. the Chinese tradition spread to Japan, where it evolved into the present-day Japanese garden.

AFTER THE FALL

When the Roman Empire collapsed, Roman gardens across the empire quickly fell into neglect. Fountains and aqueducts filled with weeds, marble terraces crumbled, topiaries reverted to sprawling thickets. In Britain, in the Roman city of Bath, unwashed Angles and Saxons wondered at the function of all those complex pipes and pools.

In Europe during the Dark Ages (c. 500–1300) monks kept alive the practice of horticulture, cultivating grape vines and fruit trees in tidy little walled plots. The flowers beloved by the Romans were now valued for their Christian symbolism: the rose signified divine love or Christ's blood; the white lily, now called the Madonna lily, purity. Periwinkle was grown to make the wreaths that were worn by condemned prisoners on the way to the gallows.

Herbs were big in the Middle Ages. Given a diet consisting chiefly of stale bread and bland porridge, with maybe a scrap of dubious meat on a feast day, a pinch or two of sage or thyme must have made a big hit with the people of that era. Herbs were also grown for their medicinal properties and, not least of all, for their fragrance, useful in a world that had ceased bathing.

Various forms of tree bondage were invented during this time: pollarding, pleaching, coppicing and the espalier. Whether this is because trees were more unruly in those days, or their keepers expected more of them, we do not know.

In England, in Tudor times (c. 1600), knot

My gardens sweet,
enclosed with
walls strong,
Embanked with
benches to sit and
take my rest;
The knots so enknot-
ted it cannot be
expressed,
With arbors and
alleys so pleasant
and so dulce,
The pestilent airs
with flavours to
repulse . . .

George Cavendish,
sixteenth century

gardens became popular. These were enclosed plots of ground in which low hedges of box or herbs like rosemary formed tortuous, knot-like patterns.

ELSEWHERE

In the rest of the world, garden fashions changed slowly. Mohammed (570–632) promised his followers an afterlife in a garden, featuring, besides the usual amenities, rivers that would run wine and honey, and beautiful houris "of resplendent beauty, blooming youth, virgin purity and exquisite sensibility." Following Islam, the Persian garden style spread across the Middle East to North Africa, east to India, and to Spain with the Moors.

In Japan, gardeners were creating landscapes of moss, raked sand and carefully placed boulders; some individual rocks were so highly valued that they were traded like stocks and even, on occasion, plundered.

Under Kublai Khan the Chinese landscape style achieved its greatest triumphs. When Marco Polo returned to Italy from Peking (c. 1300), he rhapsodized about the wonders he had seen—parks that covered eight square miles, "ornamented with many handsome

"For some miles around Adrianople the whole ground is laid out with Gardens, and the Banks of the River set with Rows of Fruit Trees, under which all the most considerable Turks divert themselves every Evening: not with walking, that is not one of their Pleasures, but a set party of 'em chuse out a green spot where the Shade is very thick, and there they spread a carpet on which they sit drinking their Coffee."

Lady Mary Wortley Montagu, in a letter to Alexander Pope, 1717 trees, and meadows in which are kept various kinds of beasts"—but made no converts. European gardens remained inside walls.

In the Americas the Mayas, Incas, Aztecs, etc., all gardened. On the site of what is now Mexico City, the great city of Tenochtitlán was built on a lake that was surrounded by vast floating gardens—among them the world's largest extant botanical garden. They were "discovered" in 1519 by Cortés, who proceeded to destroy them.

THE RENAISSANCE

Sixteenth-century Italy was in a fever of building. It was a time of surging economic prosperity, and, as always, the newly wealthy constructed elaborate garden paradises to show off their affluence.

In 1503 Pope Julius II had commissioned the architect Bramante to design gardens for the Vatican in conjunction with the reconstruction of St. Peter's. Bramante was a follower of the great architectural theorist Alberti, who in his *Ten Books on Architecture* (1452) laid out the rules for garden design according to rigid precepts borrowed from the ancient Romans. A fanatic believer in symmetry, Alberti said "Trees ought to be planted in

"It was a good agreeable piece of flattery among the ancient gardeners to trace their masters' names in box, or in sweet-smelling herbs in parterres. Rose trees, intermixed with pomegranates and cornels, are very beautiful in a hedge. . . . what we are told Democritus very much condemned, namely, the inclosing of a garden with any sort of wall, I should not blame in the case before us but am rather of the opinion, that it is very proper defense against malice or rapine. Nor am I displeased with the placing of ridiculous statues in gardens, provided they have nothing in them obscene."

Leon Battista Alberti , Ten Books on Architecture, *1452*

*Here a Chimera
opens wide his
jaws
And from his mouth
a torrent
throws . . .
There with his arms,
and watching as
his game
A brazen huntsman
stands and takes
his aim,
To kill the prey, but
shoots a harmless
stream;
A pleasing cheat,
at which the
wond'ring rout,
At once with Laugh-
ter and applauses
shout.*

René Rapin,
"Of Gardens,"
1666

rows exactly even and answering to one an-other exactly in straight lines."

In the lush countryside outside Rome, wealthy noblemen and princes of the Church spent fortunes building magnificent garden villas. Architecture took first place in these designs; trees and plants were secondary, and were expected to behave as if sculpted of stone. Water was especially important; in the Renaissance it was made to do things it had never done before and probably never will again. At the Villa d'Este in Tivoli, an entire river was rechanneled to supply an elaborate series of waterworks; one of the many terraces alone contains 100 fountains.

The classic Renaissance garden was on a hill, with terraces descending along a central axis. Grand staircases linked the different lev-els, with water flowing from terrace to terrace by means of complex fountains and cascades. Flowers, though admired, had to mind their p's and q's; they were grown in pots, to be lined up along a balustrade. There were no lawns. The level terraces were stone or gravel, or filled with parterres, in which low hedges of boxwood were grown in geometric patterns designed to be appreciated from above. Statu-ary played a major role, not surprising when one considers what was available: Bramante's Vatican gardens contained, among others, the Apollo Belvedere and the Laocoön.

Alberti's austere principles didn't outlast the sixteenth century. As the Renaissance gave way to the Baroque period, the Italian villas would acquire ever more fanciful and elaborate features—labyrinths, grottoes and pergolas; here a nymphaeum, there a *giardino segreto* (a walled secret garden where romance or contemplation could be pursued in private). One estate—the Villa d'Este—boasted a complete scale model of ancient Rome, on the banks of a miniature Tiber.

A nobleman who wanted to be known as a person of consequence might commission some *automata*. In 1670 an English traveler (John Evelyn), visiting the Villa Aldobrandini, noted "hydraulic organs and all sorts of singing birds, moving and chirping by the force of water," and "the representation of a storm . . . with such fury of rain, wind and thunder as one could imagine oneself in some extreme tempest."

One of the oddest gardens was—and still is—the Villa Orsini at Bomarzo, the Disneyland of its day. Here colossal statues of grotesque animals and mythological creatures,

"You who roam the world in search of sublime and fearful wonders, come hither and look upon terrible countenances, elephants, lions, bears, man-eaters, and dragons."

Stone inscription at the entrance to Bomarzo

33

carved out of boulders, cavort about the grounds, acting out some as yet unknown allegory.

No grand Italian garden was complete without its *giochi d'acqua,* or water jokes. A favorite prank was to conceal a sprinkler inside a garden seat; the weary visitor would sink into a bench only to have his pants soaked, while his noble host crackled with mirth. At the Villa Lante, guests would be led into an enclosed garden where concealed water jets would drench them to the skin.

Many of these gardens can be seen today, in various stages of disrepair and romantic ruin. The fountains rarely work as well as they did in their heyday. (One is safe from water jokes.)

FRANCE

In 1533 the thirteen-year-old Catherine de Medici went to France to marry the future Henry II, bringing with her the arts and refinements of Italian culture. (We have her to thank for French cuisine.) She initiated many horticultural projects, including the Jardins des Tuileries in Paris.

On French soil the Italian Renaissance style soon took on a formality and a scale that it had never known at home, employing symmetry to a degree that would have delighted Alberti's orderly soul.

There were fountains and terraces as in Italy, but in the Ile de France's rolling landscape the spaces were horizontal, not vertical. These were gardens on a heroic scale, better seen on horseback than on foot; elephant back would be best. Vast *parterres de broderie*—descendants of the humble knot gardens of the Middle Ages—swept to the horizon, bordered by miles-long *allées* of lime trees, pruned into rectangles. Hidden in niches behind the *allées* were *bosquets,* intimate groves containing statues and fountains, which became the subjects for paintings by Fragonard and Boucher.

The premiere name in French garden history, André Le Nôtre, was born in a building in the Tuileries in 1613, the descendant of two generations of court horticulturists. Le Nôtre designed many splendid gardens, the greatest of them all being those at Versailles. Originally the site of one of Louis XIII's hunting lodges, Versailles was where Louis XIV—the Sun King—chose to build the grand palace in which he would consolidate his power.

"A fine Garden is no less difficult to contrive and order well than a good Building. . . . A Man should know something of geometry and architecture, and be able to draw well; he should understand ornament, be acquainted with the properties and effects of all the plants made use of in fine gardens; should design readily; and with all this, have a right judgement and natural good taste, form'd upon the contemplation of things that are excellent, the censuring of those that are ill."

Alexandre Le Blond,
The Theory &
Practice of
Gardening, *1709*

"Le Nôtre was one of the people Louis XIV liked best in the world. . . . He had a perfectly direct natural manner and never minded disagreeing with his master. . . .
He offered Le Nôtre a coat of arms but the idea was treated with derision: 'I've got one already, three slugs crowned with cabbage leaves.'

Le Nôtre hated flowers as much as the King loved them. He greatly objected to the parterres which he was obliged to plant in front of the royal palaces, saying they were fit for nursery maids to look at, out of the upper windows."

Nancy Mitford
The Sun King

Le Nôtre spent over twenty years on the vast project, with as many as 36,000 men working at one time. This was gardening on a scale such as the world had never seen. Hills were added to the essentially flat landscape to provide vistas; then the marshes were drained, and water brought in by aqueducts to fill the canals and pools and lakes, and the 1,400 fountains. (But despite all efforts, Versailles still suffers from a chronic water shortage.) The main axis of the garden runs east to west, beginning at the King's personal chamber— as though he truly were the sun—and extending to the horizon. In Versailles' heyday, 150,000 plants were grown annually to fill the parterres and planters.

There were fountains that played music, fountains that balanced balls on their jets, fountains in the form of trees. There were water jokes: "an ignoble form of humor," groused Henry James on his Grand Tour, several hundred years later. The Grand Canal was big enough for the King to use to stage mock naval battles. No wonder Horace Walpole called Versailles "the gardens of a great child"!

The French style spread across Europe. The idea of a garden as a peaceful refuge from life's aggravations was lost forever; gardens became an exercise in pretentiousness, their sole purpose the out-doing of one's neighbors. From Hampton Court to Saint Peters-burg, every monarch coveted his own Versailles. Peter the Great's palace, the Peterhof (begun in 1714), had *allées, bosquets,* and 173 fountains—including three water jokes.

Over the years, as fashions changed, Versailles underwent many transformations. Louis XV contributed a menagerie and a botanical garden, both of which were removed later. Chinese pagodas and Greek temples came and went. On the eve of the Revolution, Marie Antoinette made her mark on garden history by putting in a model peasant village with thatched cottages and a dairy, where the Queen and her coterie could play at being milkmaids and shepherds—while beyond the gates real peasants plotted their bloody downfall.

The other great French style is the *potager,* or kitchen garden, where flowers and vegetables and espaliered fruit trees grow in tidy closely planted rows and the art of treillage transforms every verti-cal surface into a plant support. Here, too, Versailles set the pace: the Potager du Roi, laid out by La Quintinie (c. 1680), covered twenty acres and contained twenty-nine walled enclosures, where all kinds of produce—edible and ornamental—was grown to sat-isfy the royal appetite.

THE NETHERLANDS

The Dutch response to the Italian and French styles of garden-ing was limited by the fact that most of Holland is flatter than a tabletop and below sea level. It is also a very small country.

However, there was plenty of money in Holland in the six-teenth and seventeenth centuries, and with it the Dutch contrived their inimitable garden style. It involved cramming great numbers of plants, topiaries, statues, fountains, urns, paths and trellises, into handkerchief-size plots. (The twentieth-century miniature golf course owes a lot to the Dutch.) Here the parterre took on new meaning; intricate scrolls and arabesques were laid out, and when plants couldn't be made to stay within their rigid bounds, they were replaced with colored sand, crushed glass and coal dust.

Of course, one cannot think of Holland without thinking of the great Tulip Mania of the 1630s: not the only occasion of a garden fad becoming a widespread obsession, but the best known.

Tulips were unknown in Europe until the winter of 1554, when an Austrian nobleman traveling through Turkey was captivated by the sight of great fields of flowers: narcissi, hyacinths, anemones and, above all, tulips. Brought to Europe, the tulips caught on quickly, and soon Dutch plantsmen were cultivating them—and selling them.

In the early 1600s it was noticed that some tulips would "break"; that is, the color would streak or craze, causing bizarre variations. Breaking is caused by a virus, which the Dutch breeders soon learned to harness.

". . . those high prices one hears about, paid for work of painters who are dead and who were never paid so much while they were alive, it is a kind of tulip trade, under which the living painters suffer. . . . And it will also disappear like the tulip trade.

But . . . though the tulip trade has long been gone and is forgotten, the flower growers have remained and will remain."

Vincent van Gogh, in a letter to his mother, 1889

(Although this has a sinister ring to it, the virus actually causes no harm to either the tulip or the breeder.) As tulips took on new shapes and colors, collectors themselves became crazed, trading the bulbs for ever escalating prices. Fortunes were made and lost. Inevitably the bubble burst, the market collapsed, and the tulip speculators lost their shirts.

Deservedly, I say. Who in his right mind would pay "two loads of wheat; four loads of rye; four fat oxen; eight fat pigs; twelve fat sheep; two hogsheads of wine; four barrels of eight-florin beer; two barrels of butter; one thousand pounds of cheese; a complete bed; a suit of clothes and a silver beaker" for one tulip bulb: for something that *might die?*

ENGLAND

The English have always been dedicated gardeners. That moist climate, where it is always either about to start or cease to rain, is ideally suited to growing a great range of plants. But until the early 1700s there was no native British style. Italian extravagance, French formality and Dutch intricacy had each been adopted in turn, and sometimes combined to bewildering effect, under the tutelage of a series of architects

His gardens next your admiration call,
On any side you look, behold the wall!
No pleasing intricacies intervene,
No artful wildness to perplex the scene;
Grove nods at grove, each ally has a brother,
And half the platform just reflects the other.
The suffering eye inverted Nature sees,
Trees cut to statues, statues thick as trees;
With here a fountain, never to be play'd;
And there a summerhouse, that knows no shade . . .

Alexander Pope,
Moral Essays,
1735

39

"Writers who have given us an account of China, tell us the inhabitants of that country laugh at the plantations of our Europeans, which are laid out by the rule and line; because, they say, any one may place trees in equal rows and uniform figures. They choose rather to show a genius in works of this nature, and therefore always conceal the art by which they direct themselves. . . . Our British gardeners, on the contrary, instead of humoring nature, love to deviate from it as much as possible. Our trees rise in cones, globes and pyramids. We see the marks of the scissors upon every plant and bush."

Joseph Addison, in the Spectator, June 1712

and designers imported from the Continent.

Then the English discovered Nature.

Suddenly, around 1700, gardening became the subject of fevered intellectual debate; it took the British to turn the garden into something to *argue about.* It began with a thorough rejection of the imported styles then in vogue, and a passion for all things natural. Addison and Steele filled the pages of the *Spectator* with essays on the subject. Alexander Pope pumped out rhymed couplets by the yard, mocking the geometric gardens of his contemporaries and pleading the "genius of the place" as the only true source of inspiration.

"Nature," pronounced William Kent, one of the first of the new garden designers, "abhors a straight line." A pseudo-Chinese word—*sharawadgi*—was coined to denote the imagined qualities of Oriental landscaping.

Before then, no one in the West had paid much attention to either nature or the landscape. Nature was rough and threatening; something to be tamed. Vistas might be enjoyed on a trip to Switzerland, but back home folks didn't want to have to gaze at anything farther away than the garden wall. Artists painted landscapes only as incidental backdrops to their subjects; the word "landscape" didn't even enter the language until the seventeenth century. The Chinese had been enjoying nature, both in painted landscapes and in the raw, for millennia, but Europeans remained mostly ignorant of those accomplishments. Nowadays, of course, gardeners compare themselves with nature all the time, but in seventeenth-century England it was a radical idea.

All of that came to an end with the invention of the ha-ha. The ha-ha is, simply, a ditch at the edge of a lawn or meadow; its purpose is to keep cows from climbing into the garden, and it is still used in this way on very large English estates. From a distance it is invisible, making for an unbroken view; the ha-ha extended the garden out to the

Consult the genius of the place in all;
That tells the waters or to rise, or fall,
Or helps th'ambitious hill the heavens to scale
Or scoops in circling theatres the vale;
Calls in the country, catches op'ning glades,
Joins willing woods, and varies shades from shades;
Now breaks, or now directs, th'intending lines,
Paints as you plant, and as you work, designs.

Alexander Pope, from "Epistle to Lord Burlington," 1728

" 'I wish you could see Compton, said he; "it is the most complete thing! I never saw a place so altered in my life . . . The approach, now, is one of the finest things in the country. You see the house in the most surprising manner. I declare, when I got back to Sotherton yesterday, it looked like a prison, quite a dismal old prison.'

'Oh, for shame!' cried Mrs Norris. 'A prison indeed? Sotherton Court is the noblest old place in the world.'

'It wants improvement, ma'am, beyond anything. I never saw a place that wanted so much improvement in my life; and it is so forlorn that I do not know what can be done with it . . .' "

Jane Austen
Mansfield Park

horizon. It is also sometimes not very visible up close, hence its name: "ha-ha!" is what one exclaims upon stumbling into one, in polite society.

Charles Bridgeman, royal gardener until his death in 1738, was the first to use the ha-ha in landscaping. Some of the other famous practitioners of the new art of landscape design—or "improvers," as they were also called—were Pope's friend William Kent, of whom Horace Walpole said, "He leaped the fence and saw all nature was a garden"; Humphrey Repton; and Lancelot "Capability" Brown, so nicknamed because he always saw the capabilities of a site.

The improvers proceeded to rearrange the English countryside. Formal Italian and French gardens were ripped out ("vandalism," according to later critics); topiaries, parterres, terraces and fountains were banished. The great English contribution to horticulture, the grass lawn, came into its own. Rivers were rerouted to take on the requisite serpentine configuration, hills were leveled or raised, trees moved from here to there, all in the name of Nature.

A generation later, much of the improver's work was itself torn up.

Eighteenth-century Englishmen visiting the Continent on Grand Tours fell in love with the "sublime" scenery of the Alps, the crumbling ruins of Rome, and with the romantic landscape paintings of Claude Lorrain and Salvator Rosa. Returning home, they looked at Capability Brown's natural landscapes and noticed that they were dull. Fashion now demanded of its gardens that they be exciting.

Now the watchword was *picturesque*. Precipices and chasms were in, serpentine was out. Dead trees were preferred to living ones. Ruins were the rage: if you didn't happen to have a crumbling Gothic castle in the backyard, you had one built. Soon the countryside was rife with grottoes and follies of every description. There was a brief vogue for hermitages with real hermits living in them, like living garden statues. One noble house had to fire its hermit after a few weeks when he was discovered breaking his vows of silence and abstinence at the local pub.

The picturesque style was short-lived, doomed by its own excesses. A revolutionary new idea was gaining adherents—the idea that the plants themselves might have a say in their display.

"English landscape was invented by gardeners imitating foreign painters who were evoking classical authors. The whole thing was brought home in the luggage from the grand tour."

from Tom Stoppard's play Arcadia

43

" 'Tis true the
Countrie hath no
Bonerets, or Tartar-
lands, no glittering
coloured Tulpes; but
here you have the
American mary-gold,
the earth- nut . . .
blue flower-de-luce,
red lilies all over the
country, dragons,
skunk cabbage,
pitcher plants, yellow
bastard Daffodils,
white hellebore,
one-berry, Bishop
Compton's sweet fern
. . . and tobacco."

John Josselyn, in
An Account of
Two Voyages to
New England,
1673

NEW PLANTS: NEW WORLDS

The first Europeans to explore the New World were astonished to find plants that were nothing like the ones at home. As religious Christians, they believed that the number of biological species must be limited to those that had survived the Flood with Noah. But once they got over their astonishment they realized that they had found a gold mine.

As New World plants like corn and potatoes crossed the ocean to find a place on the European table, others made the trip to provide curiosities for public and private gardens. Plants became *collectible.* Botanical oddities from the Americas and—as other explorers ventured elsewhere—the Orient soon filled European gardens.

Amateur and professional scientists flocked to the far corners of the world in search of new species. Some of them won immortality through their discoveries. Leonhard Fuchs gave us the fuchsia; John Tradescant, the tradescantia. These were intrepid adventurers: David Douglas (of Douglas fir fame), an accident-prone Scot who botanized in a kilt, and who survived fevers, falls, near drownings and Indian attacks, finally died in 1834 when he fell into a bull pit in

Hawaii and was attacked by an enraged beast.

The new plants called for different kinds of settings. Gardeners, always eager to outdo one another, strived to create authentic backgrounds for the plants they collected. Soon every great estate boasted a mock-Himalayan hillside, to show off a prize collection of rhododendrons; a pinetum for American conifers; an *orangerie,* in which citrus trees took shelter over the winter; a rockery for alpines. To keep the plants company, pagodas, temples and other exotic fancies followed them. This museum-like approach to gardening, with specimen trees planted singly so they could be studied from all sides, eventually acquired the graceless name of *gardenesque.*

At Malmaison, in her *jardin anglais,* Empress Josephine assembled a vast collection of plants, many of them souvenirs of Napoleon's campaigns. Acacias from Africa mingled with eucalyptus from Australia, and magnolia trees from China met magnolias from North

"Yea in May you shall see woods and fields so curiously bedecked in innumerable multitudes of delightful flowers, not only pleasing to the eye but smell, that you may hold nature contending with the arts and striving to equal if not excel many a garden in England."

Daniel Denton, "Brief Description of New York," 1670

45

America. Josephine is best known for her roses, and for the exquisite paintings that her botanical artist, Redouté, made of them. (After the divorce in 1809, Napoleon had many of the plants ripped out on the grounds that they were too English.)

In North America, European settlers had by then been gardening for a couple of centuries; and if building a garden was not the first priority for those brave—or foolhardy—souls, it followed soon after. In little fenced plots along the eastern seaboard, the colonists grew vegetables and flowers and medicinal herbs, at first from seeds brought from home, then gradually including the strange new varieties they found in the new land. In style, these plots owed more to the herbaries of the Middle Ages than they did to Bramante or Le Nôtre.

To the Atlantic trade in valuable botanical specimens, there soon was added a considerable traffic in nuisance species. Before the seventeenth century was out, European weeds—among them dandelions, burdock, Scotch thistle and wild daisy—had been released on the American continent, some accidentally, some on purpose. From Asia came other pests: Japanese honeysuckle, the common multiflora rose, and kudzu, "the vine that ate the South," deliberately introduced for purposes of erosion control—for which it is less than useless. (Unfairly, that great American native, poison ivy, has never gained a foothold on any other continent.)

As the colonists prospered, their gardens became more elaborate. In Williamsburg, Virginia, formal terraces were laid out (c. 1690) in the currently fashionable Anglo-Dutch style. Then, a generation after they revolutionized the English landscape, the naturalistic theories of Kent and Brown made their way to North

America. At Mount Vernon, George Washington mixed styles, installing formal flower beds next to his house, with serpentine avenues sweeping away to the Potomac.

Thomas Jefferson always claimed to be a farmer first; statesman, architect, scientist, philosopher and what have you, second. This is a man who grew Indian corn in his garden in Paris, while serving as minister to France (1785–89); who engaged in yearly competitions with his Virginia neighbors as to which would bring the first English pea to the table each spring.

At Monticello (Italian for "little mountain"), his 5,000-acre estate in Virginia, Jefferson laid out a *ferme ornée*—an ornamental farm—in which he combined "the articles of husbandry with the attributes of a garden," freely adapting ideas he had picked up in his travels. The building itself was Palladian. There were Italianate terraces, English-inspired sweeping prospects and clumps of trees, and orchards and vineyards, and a vegetable plot that was a thousand feet long. Flower beds combined tulips and other imports with North American natives like the Virginia bluebell. Shade trees were placed strategically to provide relief from the hot American summers. Toward the end of his life, Jefferson wrote: "Too old to plant trees for my own gratification, I shall do it for posterity."

Like so many gardeners before and since, many of Jefferson's projects were unrealized. Extensive as it is, Monticello represents only a fraction of Jefferson's dream: there were to have been cascading waterfalls, a forest preserve and even a classical grotto. The farm was never successful financially, and when Jefferson died (1826) he was massively in debt.

VICTORIAN EXCESS

In the nineteenth century the glass roof was invented, making possible greenhouses of all sizes; which in turn made it possible to rear plants in vast numbers, far from their native haunts.

In England this was the era of the great Victorian country estates. Conspicuous over-consumption was the order of the day. Wealthy landowners assembled collections of exotic trees, which they crammed into their grounds with little thought for taste or style. The parterre was back in fashion, now massed with geraniums and salvias and heliotropes in vivid primary colors. It was said that the rich "used to show their wealth by the size of their bedding plant list: ten thousand for a squire, twenty for a baronet, thirty for an earl and forty for a duke."

Meanwhile, in America, fabulously wealthy robber barons were building estates on a scale to rival their British counterparts. Freely and unblushingly borrowing ideas, they created lavish confections in a pastiche of styles.

In Newport, William Kissam Vanderbilt's Marble House, patterned after the Petit Trianon at Versailles, has an actual Chinese tea-

"By the mid-nineteenth century eclecticism had destroyed the growth or continuance of style and the 'museum' age was well started. Revival followed revival. Each country reconstructed lavish replicas: Renaissance, Louis XV, Tudor. Far removed in time and in thought from the makers of the original gardens, architects and designers wallowed in a sea of superficialities, and the essential weakness of their concepts was accentuated by indiscriminate planting."

Russell Page
The Education of a
Gardener

house in its otherwise Italian gardens. The Stanford White-designed Naumkeag (from an Indian word meaning "place of rest") in Stockbridge, Massachusetts, also contains chinoiserie, along with sweeping staircases reminiscent of the Villa d'Este. In Pasadena, California, the Huntington family installed formal rosebeds, a medieval knot garden, a desert environment, a tropical rain forest, and a Japanese sand-and-rock garden on their grounds; inside, the estate's treasures included Gainsborough's *Blue Boy* and a Gutenberg Bible.

It was the last gasp of the grandiose.

"A SIMPLE AND TENDER CHARM"

By the end of the nineteenth century both Europe and America had thriving nursery industries. Not only squires and dukes and robber barons and ex-presidents, but ordinary homeowners with quarter-acre lots gardened. And for city folk, who couldn't have garden edens of their own, the first public parks were built. With more people becoming horticulturally inclined, attitudes changed.

Grand-scale carpet bedding is, to put it mildly, labor intensive. Both it and the gardenesque style, with its carefully nurtured specimen plants standing like statues in a sea of cropped lawn, require lots of land and armies of workers, pricing them way out of reach of ordinary homeowners. But impracticability isn't what doomed these styles; what did them in was the fact that they weren't pretty.

Along the country lanes of England, cottagers grew old-fashioned flowers—hollyhocks and stock and sweet peas—in charming

49

"A gentleman's park is what I abhor. It is not beauty because it is not nature."

John Constable

profusion. These gardens were *pretty*; artists painted them. An Irish writer, William Robinson, in a number of books beginning with *The Wild Garden* (1871), praised these humble, artless plots and fulminated against carpet bedding, topiary, statuary, and artificiality of all sorts. Once again Nature was called upon to save the garden.

Gertrude Jekyll (1843–1932) was originally a disciple of William Robinson. A Victorian spinster of formidable energy and fierce opinions, she was an artist as well as a writer and garden designer. "The little strips in front of roadside cottages," she said, "have a simple and tender charm that one may look for in vain in gardens of greater pretensions."

Jekyll is the mother of the modern perennial border, the first to advocate planting in "drifts." She was severely myopic, and it has been suggested that there is a relationship between her blurred vision and the blurry drifts of color she advocated. (The same has been said of Monet, another myopic artist-gardener.) It is certainly true that many Jekyll-inspired gardens look best when one scrinches up one's eyes, simulating myopia.

Jekyll and Robinson did not see entirely eye to eye; Robinson was against formality of any sort, while Jekyll advocated strong architectural underpinnings—what the style writers call "good bones." She and the architect Sir Edwin Lutyens (1869– 1944) collaborated on many projects around the world, in which his bold frameworks set off her lush plantings. Jekyll is still very influential today, as much in the United States as in her own country; each generation of gardeners rediscovers—or reinvents—her. It is probably not fair to blame her for the popular misconception that a romantic cottagey border of sweetly scented heirloom blooms is an easy thing to create.

In their garden at Sissinghurst Castle, Vita Sackville-West and her husband, Harold Nicolson, took Jekyll's humble cottage garden and upgraded it, thus transforming Robinson's naturalism into a new kind of formalism. Nicolson was an important statesman and a biographer, Sackville- West a successful novelist and poet; together and separately they led a sometimes scandalous—though happy—private life, but it is for the gardens that they are best remembered. Sissinghurst was a near ruin in 1930 when they bought it, a collection of falling-down towers and buildings dating to the sixteenth century. Over a period of thirty years they created what is now the most

". . . Whenever I have seen the large formal gardens attached to important houses of the Palladian type that are so numerous throughout England, I have always been struck by their almost invariable lack of interest and want of any real beauty or power of giving happiness. . . . I hold the firm belief that the purpose of a garden is to give happiness and repose of mind . . . through the representation of the best kind of pictorial beauty of flower and foliage that can be combined or invented.

I always suppose that these great wide dull gardens, sprawling over much too large a space, are merely an outgrowth of plan drawing."

Gertrude Jekyll

51

*"Never has Sissing-
hurst looked more
lovely or been more
appreciated. I must
say, Farley has made
the place look like a
gentleman's garden,
and you with your
extraordinary taste
have made it look
like nobody's garden
but your own. . . .
Then I think, si j'ose
m'exprimer ainsi,
that the design is
really rather good.
I mean we have got
what we wanted to
get—a perfect pro-
portion between the
classical and the
romantic, between the
element of expectation
and the element of
surprise. . . . it is
lovely, lovely, lovely
—and you must be
pleased with your
work."*

*Harold Nicolson,
in a letter to Vita
Sackville-West,
1937*

famous and, possibly, the most beautiful garden in England.

The gardens—among them the renowned
White Garden—are tucked in between the
ancient walls, planted according to Sackville-
West's philosophy: "Profusion, even extravagance and exuberance, within the confines of
the utmost linear severity." While much of the
heavy work was done by paid help, Vita took
part in every aspect of the project—so much so
that her friend Virginia Woolf complained that
she had become an unkempt and overweight
countrywoman, whose only interests were
"dogs, flowers and new buildings."

After Nicolson's and Sackville-West's deaths,
Sissinghurst was taken over by the National
Trust and is now one of Britain's most popular tourist attractions, up there with Bucking-
ham Palace and Stonehenge. A staff of six
full-time gardeners tends its six acres.

SUBURBIA

In America the democratization of gardening, begun in the nineteenth century with
the rise of large-scale plant culture, took off
with a bang in the twentieth. New methods of
hybridizing, chemicals that promised to eliminate pests and diseases, mechanized gizmos

for tilling and mowing, all encouraged a sky's-the-limit attitude. Now even ordinary folk could hope to grow the first blue rose, the world's biggest pumpkin. Garden clubs and *The Guinness Book of Records* encouraged these dreams.

Meanwhile grand-scale gardening, which had gone from Nebuchadnezzar's Hanging Gardens through the Italian Renaissance to achieve its finest moments in eighteenth-century France, died a slow, whimpering death, doomed by the Depression and World War II. (Which is not to say that pretentiousness had ceased to exist on the earth.)

After the Second World War vast numbers of suddenly affluent middle-class families swarmed to America's suburbs, many of them to brand-new developments and to a life-style without historical precedent; in fact, the concept of "life style" was itself so new it used up two words. For the new suburbanites, having one's own personal backyard eden came to seem one of those inalienable rights guaranteed by the Constitution.

Naturalism had found, shall we say, fertile ground. Americans were not comfortable

"It is unchristian to hedge from the sight of others the beauties of nature which it has been our good fortune to create or secure; and all the walls, high fences, hedge screes and belts of trees and shrubbery which are used for that purpose only, are so many means by which we show how unchristian and unneighborly we can be."

Frank J. Scott,
in The Art
of Beautifying
Suburban Home
Grounds,
1870

with the notion of a garden as a place where man imposed his will upon nature. (Although they had no problem imposing upon nature for reasons of practicality, such as cutting down a stand of virgin trees for lumber or digging up a wetland to build a shopping mall.) Formality was un-American. Stone terraces, clipped hedges and classical statuary did not belong in suburban yards—although gazing globes and plastic flamingos were right at home.

As early as 1870 Frank J. Scott, an influential landscape designer and writer, had pleaded the case for the boundary-less suburban lawn; walls and fences were, according to him, not only undemocratic but "unchristian." Said he, solemnly: "The beauty obtained by throwing front grounds together, is of that excellent quality which enriches all who take part in the exchange, and makes no man poorer."

By the middle of the twentieth century the American suburban landscape had acquired its familiar shape, recognizable from Long Island to Marin County. Wide lawns—with sprinklers laboring away—fill the space between house and road, and from house to house. Occasional trees, perhaps a blue spruce or a Japanese maple to break up the unrelenting green, dot the lawn, with curving sweeps of shrubbery or pachysandra outlining the driveway. The house itself has evergreen shrubs—yews clipped into muffin shapes—planted tightly around the foundation as if to hide its ugly ankles. (And if the house is more than twenty years old, to hide the first-floor windows too.) The landscape is soothing and restful and monochromatic, except for the few weeks in spring when the azaleas flower and the blast of color in autumn.

It is also oddly unpopulated; you can drive for hours in the suburbs without spotting a single human, other than those on lawn mowers. The humans—if they are at home at all—are in the background.

CALIFORNIA

Garden design in American backyards owes more to Japan and Spain than it does to the Roman-French-English tradition. Both influences came to America via California.

The Japanese landscape style appealed to Americans for several reasons. It looked "modern"; it suited the low ranch houses and the small suburban lots of the postwar period. Japanese plants thrived in North America, better suited to the climate than European varieties. Last but not least: although real

"Today, with the average extent of our properties lying between the fifty-foot lot and the suburban acre, any likeness between us and Louis XIV has disappeared, except that we too like to give garden parties."

Thomas Church
Gardens Are for
People

Japanese gardens require almost constant grooming, they *looked* easy to maintain. Once Americans realized how rigorous and formal the Japanese garden actually was, it ceased to be a major influence. Except for the plants and some stylistic doodads—lanterns, stone Buddhas—the only Japanese element in most suburban American gardens today is the sinuous curve of the shrubbery.

The Spanish heritage has always been strong in California gardens, with their sheltered courtyards and outdoor living spaces, and sunny arid climate. It is a tradition that reaches back through the Moors to ancient Persia. If an Italian garden is meant to be viewed from above, a French garden to be seen from a carriage and an English garden to be walked through, a Spanish garden is meant to be *lived in.*

Thomas Church was a landscape designer who worked in the 1930s and '40s. Borrowing freely from the Spanish and the Japanese, he created gardens that exemplified what was to become known as the California style. Private outdoor swimming pools (the first since the ancient Romans) became popular in California in mid-century.

Church placed them near the back door and surrounded them with naturalistic, low-maintenance plantings. Space flowed easily between house and landscape, with decks and patios mediating between. For the first time in history, outdoor furniture was designed to be comfortable, not just ornamental. Outdoor activities—croquet, tennis, badminton and the cocktail party— gained adherents. Guys learned to put on funny aprons and burn steaks over an outdoor fireplace.

Church said: "Landscaping is not a complex and difficult art to be practiced only by high priests. . . . It is logical, down-to-earth, and aimed at making your plot of ground produce exactly what you want and need from it." The title of his best-known book was *Gardens Are for People.*

Not for plants, or for history, or to set off a beautiful house, or to inspire lofty thoughts; just for *people*: a hell of an idea. In no time at all, the informal California style had conquered backyards across America and jumped the Atlantic to find adherents in Europe, especially in Scandinavia.

For a while it seemed that the People Garden was the end of the story, the happily-ever-after fulfillment of ten thousand years of garden history. Of course, it wasn't. A generation later the ungrateful people had rejected it.

One of the few outdoor pastimes *not* accommodated in Church's California paradises is, ironically, gardening. These are landscapes that are cared for by a "service," an outside contractor who mows and prunes and replaces dead plants. They are gardens that don't need gardeners.

The practice of horticulture wants a clearly defined space; you can't just tuck a few tomato plants in among the rhododendrons or next to the pool. If you do, the following year you'll want a fenced-

*"Once the crew fin-
ished planting the
shrubs and laying
down the carpet of
sod, there was noth-
ing left to do but
look at it. . . . what
it lacked most was
a garden. True, con-
sidered whole, it
was a garden, but to
my mind (as in the
common American
usage) a garden was
a small plot of flowers
or vegetables; every-
thing else was a
'yard' . . . I wanted
. . . a place where I
could put my hands
on the land and
make it do things.
. . . I wanted to
dig."*

Michael Pollan
Second Nature

off area, square or rectangular preferably, and big enough for the beans and basil and lettuce you've decided to grow also. And another square, please, for the cosmos and larkspur and snapdragons you want to raise for cutting. And one for wildflowers . . . Before you know it the backyard has filled up with a number of different spaces, almost like a series of "rooms."

GILDING THE PUMPKIN

Some time in the past quarter-century Amer-icans began actually gardening, as op-posed to just sitting in the backyard. It began in the '70s with the interest in nature and ecology and growing your own vegetables (and other substances). Then, in the '80s, the booming economy created a lot of people with more money than they'd ever had before, and a desperate need to quickly acquire the trap-pings of wealth. The New Age and the Nou-veaux Riches: talk about strange bedfellows!

The revolt against the amorphous Califor-nia landscape style paralleled that against the International style in architecture. The new gar-deners didn't want their parents' pachysandra any more than they wanted their Eames chairs or their kidney-shaped swimming pools.

They wanted old-fashioned flowers: the perennials Grandma used to grow; heirloom roses with fancy foreign names (Duchesse de Portland, Konigin von Danemark, Belle de Crecy). To go with their new Palladian windows (available at every lumberyard) they wanted stone paths, knot gardens, topiary, *treillage.* Walls, the higher and thicker the better; how about a *giardino segreto?* Suddenly formalism—which seemed like a bad joke a generation ago—looked good.

For garden rooms, and for a style that might be called Upscale Cottage Garden, Americans looked backward, to a glamorized past, and eastward, to England. They read Gertrude Jekyll; they made pilgrimages to Sissinghurst Castle and other nostalgic English sites. The fact that the Sissinghurst style is almost impossible to replicate in the United States—even if one could hire the trained staff and somehow re-create the Tudor setting, the climate just isn't appropriate—didn't make it any less desirable.

In the '90s the economic bubble—and a few others—burst. As the world beyond their property lines began to get ugly and scary, even more Americans turned to gardening. Those property lines were now likely to be wired: suburbia was increasingly patrolled by visible or invisible electronic monitors. In this, once again, California led the way. (What would Frank Scott—he who thought fences "unchristian"—have made of those "Armed Response" signs that line the roads of Beverly Hills and Palm Springs?)

In the face of all the horrendous problems of the world, growing plants seems like a virtuous and positive thing to do; a blow struck for the future of the poor old planet, as well as a passport back to a pastoral golden age. There's even the hope that gardening might make us healthier or more spiritual or at least nicer:

"If I did it, you can do it too!

You can create a beautiful home and the elegant lifestyle to go with it.

I grew up the oldest child in a family of eight with very modest means. Though I was raised to be inventive and industrious, I had no place to learn about style and sophistication. . . . When I started my garden in Westport, I was the original Brown Thumb—a know-nothing if there ever was one. Today, gardening is my passion—and that neglected wreck of waist-high weeds has become my masterpiece, my pride and joy.

I did it, and you can do it, too! . . ."

Advertising flyer for
Martha Stewart
Living

"a better person," as Martha Stewart says she has become.

To help us create our American Sissinghursts, here's the indefatigable Martha Stewart, who has made a booming career out of telling the rest of us how to live. In book after book and now a magazine, she tells us how to be Marthas; how to remake our lives in her image, creating everything from bread to potpourri to table decorations from scratch. She mines a seemingly inexhaustible vein of nostalgia—perhaps for the childhood we wish we'd had.

In *Martha Stewart's Gardening* she shows us how to take her hands-on tactics outdoors. Here she is, hair artfully out of place, feeding her chickens, dumping a load of gravel out of her quaintly rusted wheelbarrow (rust is in!), pruning her fruit trees, shepherdessing a passel of adorable tots on an Easter egg hunt, gilding her *"potirons"*—which, as we all know, is French for pumpkins.

Talk about garden rooms! Martha's Connecticut farm (there are others) boasts three Orchards (East, West and New), a formal herb garden, several rose gardens, a vast vegetable plot fenced with still more roses, perennial borders too many to count, and separate plots for sweet peas, tulips, crocus and irises. Her chickens have a chicken coop *and* a Palais des Poulets. Not since Marie Antoinette played milkmaid with sterling-silver buckets has farming been this scenic.

Waxing lyrical about compost, and letting the chickens "range free" in the vegetable plot, Martha Stewart gives the impression that she's an organic gardener; in fact, she is not. In a brisk parenthesis— "(I would prefer an entirely natural garden, but in our congested area, disease and pest control is necessary)"—she dismisses the issue. The new environmentalists wouldn't allow her in their club.

THE RETURN OF THE NATIVE

The pendulum of style, ever shifting between formalism and naturalism, has lately been swinging back and forth with the velocity of hem lengths.

A rigid and uncompromising back-to-nature movement is the newest trend. It manifests itself variously: in gardens where only wildflowers are admitted (but they mustn't be plucked from the wild); in chemical-free vegetable plots, where armies of beneficial bugs battle bad bugs in hand-to-hand (feeler-to-feeler?) combat; in an interest in Native American herbs and medicines.

Meadows are in, lawns are out. Grasses are invited into flower borders, where the black-eyed Susan is replacing the rose. Open-pollinated species are preferred over the newer hybrids. After 500 years, the practice of moving plants from one part of the world to another is now repudiated.

In California (where else?) there's a growing effort to banish all plants that are not native to the state. The eucalyptus is particularly despised. These tall, graceful trees—without which one cannot imagine San Francisco—are originally Australian and, it turns out, terrible villains. They shed, they topple over suddenly, they explode into flames. Out with them: if they have not yet been illegalized, they soon will be. (Ethnobiological cleansing, one might call it.)

To have an environmentally correct native garden, it is not enough to just sit back and let the weeds grow tall; you must, it turns out, be as aggressive as though you were attempting a Versailles.

Sara Stein, in her book *Noah's Garden,* tells us she spent ten years turning an overgrown property in Westchester County into a handsome suburban garden, only to discover that in so doing she had destroyed the ecology of her land and eliminated the habitats of the wildlife—the frogs, grouse, foxes, and various birds—that had called it home. She then spent almost as many years reversing the process, using fire, bulldozers and even herbicides to eradicate the introduced plants, which she then replaced with bona fide natives. The wildlife are coming back. But no ring-necked pheasants, please: "This beautiful import from Europe and Asia is a pest in some areas where it harasses native ground birds and compromises prairie restoration."

"The relentless spread of suburbia's neat yards and gardens has caused local extinctions of such important predators as foxes, has dangerously reduced the habitat of many kinds of birds, and has threatened the total extinction of

And no deer: the white-tailed deer—as bona fide a native as the Iroquois—are kept out of Stein's land by electric fencing. If she allowed them into her ecologically authentic yard, there might be "ominous repercussions." In nibbling on tender growth, deer destroy the foliage food of various benign caterpillars without which an entire food chain is eliminated, thus resulting in the triumph of the egregious (and non-native) gypsy moth.

One is interested but not awfully surprised to learn that in Nazi Germany there was a movement, led by none other than Heinrich Himmler, to eliminate non-native plants: "to give the German people its characteristic garden and to help guard it from unwholesome alien influences." A little woodland flower, *Impatiens parviflora,* was singled out as a target for extermination; one would like to think it has outlasted Himmler.

More and more, Nature seems like that home you can't go back to. Nevertheless, we make the effort: most everyone is organic nowadays, to some extent—though I don't notice the chemical companies going out of business.

Still, we try. We grow heirloom vegetables, order ladybugs and praying mantises

> *fragile species such as orchids that rely on a single pollinator, butterflies that require a specific host plant, songbirds that inhabit deep woods, and turtles whose routes to breeding sites are interrupted by roads or obliterated by drainage projects. Entire communities of plants and insects—the well-stocked pantry of our native countryside—have been wiped bare."*
>
> Sara Stein
> Noah's Garden

through the mail (even though in our heart of hearts we believe the only good bug is a dead one), eat our pockmarked apples and ignore the brown patches on the lawn. Snuggled into a splintery Adirondack chair, dressed in our authentic Japanese farmer's togs, an Italian market umbrella shielding us from the sun, we flip through the latest Smith & Hawken catalog looking for ideas to pull it all together. All of garden history has come down to this, to me, to now. So . . . How about a meadow? Or a lily pond, or a grotto, or a knot garden . . .

No, a meadow it is. Call the contractor, alert the landscaper, it's meadow time.

It won't last. Nothing ever does, in the garden.

MICRO-GARDENING

There are two kinds of gardeners: those who start their annuals from seed indoors in February or March, nursing them along until outdoor-planting time; and those who are content to buy seedlings at a garden center in May. For the longest time I, very sensibly, counted myself among the latter.

Oh, I may have made a stab at seed-starting once or twice. I may have bought a few packages of flower seed at the hardware store, seduced by the gaudy pictures on the front of the packet, but then I would get no further; not after reading the instructions on the back, to discover that I'd have to coddle these embryonic plants for months and months before seeing any of those pretty flowers. (Somehow one never reads the small print until one gets home.)

For years and years I no more thought of growing my own seedlings than I did of building my own furniture or making my own shoes. I enjoyed direct-seeding those plants—sunflowers, beans, radishes, etc.—that could be started outside in the garden, in spring. But indoors? No way!

My husband was the seed maven in the family. Early every spring he would commandeer all the windowsills and fill them with little tomato starts, which he would then fuss over for weeks and weeks—worrying over every failed seed, crowing at each new leaf or bud—until they were ready for life outdoors. I mostly ignored the whole business, secretly convinced that store-bought seedlings were as good or better, as cheap or cheaper.

But then a few years ago I made a sudden about-face. I now grow all kinds of annual plants from seed every spring: flowers, vegetables and herbs; so many, we need a greenhouse.

"If all you want is a half dozen petunia plants, it is more economical to buy a flat of six seedlings raised by someone else than to buy 150 seeds for roughly the same price and spend three months rearing the plants yourself."

Roger Swain
The Practical
Gardener

Why the change? Was it my burgeoning interest in botany? The wish to grow rare plant varieties, unavailable in garden centers? The urge to have a more intimate hands-on relationship with my plants? Or was it simply that, my children having grown up, I didn't have enough to worry about? That was it. I was anxiety-deficient. I missed that constant seesawing between joy and sorrow, pride and disappointment; I needed the nagging tug of guilt that comes with parenting.

Plant nurturing demands almost as much of a commitment as child nurturing. There's always something you ought to be doing, and something you're probably doing wrong. Like one's offspring, one's plants don't always turn out as expected. And as with child-raising, plant-raising has stages, with rewards and pitfalls at each step along the way.

GETTING READY

Okay. You're going to do it. You're going to create a garden from . . . dots. The callused hands and strong back that serve you so well outside, busting sod and heaving bales of manure and mulch, won't be needed now. But you will need strong legs, because you'll be spending long hours on your feet. Instead of shovels and pitchforks, you'll be using lilliputian implements: toothpicks, tweezers, table silver. You'll also want keen eyesight and dextrous fingers, the kinds of skills more usually required of surgeons than of gardeners.

You'll need money, too. You'll have to buy seeds, of course; that's the fun part. Also the cheap part. Seeds aren't very expensive, even if—even though—you go completely crazy and buy enough of them to solve world hunger. What costs money is all those necessary *things*: little pots or flats or seed-starting kits, of which there is a bewildering variety to choose from. You'll need dirt—excuse me, seed-starting mix—to put in the pots, and trays to put the pots on. Then there's the question of where to put all those little wanna-be plants: Is there enough sunlight on that windowsill? Is it warm enough? Maybe you should spring for a kit, with lights and shelves and an automatic timer to control the lights. How about an electric heating pad to keep the soil at optimum temperature? What about a watering system . . . ?

This is the point where you might reconsider, decide to put all that energy and money into something else: learning ancient Greek, perhaps, or taking a round-the-world cruise. Instead of which you stand there in the kitchen, mixing batches of soil according to some arcane formula—so much peat, so much vermiculite, so much water.

TIMING

You can't just start planting your seeds at any old time; there are Rules. Petunias, for example, should be started "6–10 weeks before last frost" (Burpee). So how do you estimate a "last frost"? Even if you remembered the date of last year's last frost, you'd still be in the dark about this year's. So you decide on an arbitrary date—May 15 in my zone—and count back. Six to ten weeks allows me lots of leeway, possibly *too* much; from April 2 to March 5. If I estimate wrongly, I may be stuck with leggy overgrown seedlings that are ready for the garden long before the garden is ready for them or, worse yet, immature plants that won't flower until summer's nearly over.

With tomato seed they tell you to get them started "6 weeks before plants can be safely set in the ground without danger of frost" (Johnny's Selected Seeds). The spectre of a late frost blighting my baby seedlings is so horrific, I may delay starting my tomato seed until the beginning of May! With leek seeds one is on less shifty ground: they can be started any time as long as it's *early.*

PLANTING

The time has come to plant the little fellows. Handling a first batch of seeds, one feels clumsy and absurdly out-scaled. It's hard to believe that those tiny, inert specks will ever amount to anything; they're so little they get lost in the palm of one's hand. Sneeze and the entire summer's harvest is lost forever.

While some seeds will thrive no matter what, others have exacting requirements: "plant ½ inch deep, ½ inch apart"; "¼ inch deep, ½ inch apart." Some need light to germinate, while others prefer to be kept in the dark. Those petunia seeds want to be just barely covered with dirt; plant them too deep and they won't grow, they'll just lie there sulking until they rot.

The leek instructions seem simple enough: "Sow in flats in Feb.–Mar., ¼ inch apart, ¼ inch deep" (Johnny's). I fill a "flat"—a shallow plastic tray with drainage holes—with whatever blend of seed-starting dirt I've decided upon, moisten it and wait (a long time) for the excess water to drain out. While I wait, I make labels that say something like "King Richard Leeks, 2/19." I've tried sticking little toothpick flags into the pots with labels attached, and I've tried using stick-on labels and attaching them to the pots, and I've tried writing on plastic tags with a laundry marker; none of them has worked out really well. But I keep labeling because otherwise I'd have no idea what I'd planted.

Now I get to work, poking quarter-inch

"I presume some method is known and practiced with you to make the seeds [of Juniper] come up. I have never known but one person succeed with them here. He crammed them down the throats of his poultry confined in the hen-yard and then sowed their dung, which has been completely effectual."

Thomas Jefferson, in a letter to Mme. de Tesse, 1805

holes in the dirt with a toothpick and dropping the little seeds inside. An hour later I'm
still at it: my shoulders have stiffened into a
painful hunch, my hand is clenched on the
toothpick in a death grip, all circulation in
my legs has ceased, my eyes ache from the
continual strain—and there's no end in sight.
That small paper packet contains an inexhaustible number of leek seeds; three hundred, to be exact.

Eventually I run out, either of seeds or of
patience. I cover the flat with a sheet of plastic wrap to keep it from drying out, put it in
a warm spot—and wait.

GERMINATION

It's the miracle of life itself: those little dry
brown specks of matter swell and split and
send forth a tiny stem, which then pushes
its way to the surface, there to grow into
the petunia plant—or tomato vine, or leek—
of your dreams.

Unfortunately, not every seed germinates
without help. Some need to be soaked or nicked
or frozen or cooked or otherwise abused, to
coax them into life. Some are simply duds, as
lifeless as they look. And then there are the
slow ones; they can take weeks to sprout, and

*"[To germinate pars-
ley seeds:] Place
seeds on a sheet of
sandpaper and rub
them with another
piece of sandpaper as
vigorously as possible
(without losing
the seed). Then freeze
the seeds for a week.
Just before planting,
pour boiling water
over the seed."*

Shelley Goldbloom
Garden Smarts

during this time, the pots must be kept moist, warm and protected.

It's an anxious time for the gardener: sneaking peeks under the plastic blanket on an hourly basis; moving the tray from room to room in search of the ideal temperature; worrying if the flat is too wet/not wet enough, if the seeds were planted too deep/not deep enough.

Nowhere in all the flood of verbiage in the catalogs is there information on how much time a given seed might take to germinate. (Although the package always gives a *germination rate,* something like "70% avg germ," a number of very little usefulness.) It would be nice to know, for instance, that if my petunias haven't cracked the surface after ten days I should write them off and replant. You're left staring at an expanse of unbroken dirt, with not a clue as to what is or is not happening underground.

Sometimes—and this is almost worse than having no seeds come up—a *few* come up. There you are with four leeks out of the three hundred you planted. The ones that sprouted need sunlight to grow, and for their sake you must remove that plastic cover; however, the laggards (assuming they're viable) still need darkness and moisture.

INFANCY

Usually, though, seeds do come up (or why else bother with them?), and it is a thrilling sight indeed to see those frail little green stems, bravely wearing their starter foliage.

These newborn plants, like babies everywhere, have a host of demands that must be met, *or else.*

Right away they need light, and lots of it. Your sunniest window is barely bright enough; fluorescent lights may be a better choice. Of course, you'll have to find some way of keeping the trays at the right distance from the lights: close but not actually touching.

They need water—just the right amount. Those shallow flats and potlets usually dry out so quickly that daily watering is essential. (Don't plan a vacation this month.) Naturally, you have to water gently, so the wee seedlings don't wash away; it's best to water them from the bottom, but you must never *never* let them sit in a puddle. Too much water leads to mildew and fungus and the dread "damping off" disease, all of which give them an excuse to die.

They'll need a bit of fertilizer, maybe some of that smelly fish stuff: just a bit, though; give them too much and it's curtains. They also need air circulating around them; add an electric fan to your materiel list.

Temperature is important, too; over eighty degrees and they wilt, under fifty and most garden annuals stop growing. With melons, it's best to "Hold temperature about 75" (Johnny's). Hang the cost: turn the thermostat up.

THINNING

Despite all our efforts at planting seeds "½ inch apart," they all somehow come up in a tangle: three hundred threadlike leeks in the same one inch of soil. They cannot grow like this; you must thin them. Three weeks ago they were inanimate bits of matter and then you gave them life. Now you're supposed to annihilate half of them, ruthlessly toss them away as though they were weeds. At least when I raised my children nobody ever told me to thin them.

TRANSPLANTING

Several weeks after Thinning comes Transplant time, yet another intermediate stage in the growing-up process—like junior high school.

I dread this job. It involves carefully lifting each little bitty plant by a leaf (never by the stem!) and disentangling it from its fellows without damaging or breaking any of those translucent stems or losing any hairlike roots—never have one's hands seemed so big and clumsy—then gently (but firmly, always firmly) tucking it into a new pot, where it can grow solo until it's time for the next traumatic separation. (Unless you've killed it, which is always a strong possibility.) It is a thoroughly unnerving experience. Once done, both plant and planter need a good drink, but the planter must repeat the procedure with each one of the perhaps hundreds of little seedlings in the flat.

Not all the annuals one raises from seed need to go through this step. Many—lettuce, melons, most flowers—can go on growing in the pots or flats they germinated in, until they're ready to move into the garden. On the other hand, many experts recommend transplanting tomatoes *twice.*

ADOLESCENCE

By now trays of seedlings fill your house like an occupying army: three hundred pots of leeks in the kitchen, thirty-six tomato plants in the living room, shar-ing shelf space with one hundred snapdragons . . . (Many of these iden-tifications are guesswork, as those labels you painstakingly made are now hopelessly blurred and illegible.) You're spending an hour or more a day watering plants, and another hour mov-ing them around so they all can have equal access to the light.

Some of the plants have died, a thing seedlings do with stunning abruptness. Of the sur-vivors some, despite all your ef-forts, have grown tall and spindly, with wide spaces between the leaves; some so tall they flop over. A few of the tomatoes and peppers may already have little buds or even fruit on them, and this is *not* a good thing. Steel yourself: you've got to pinch off those flowers and fruit. Premature fruiting is a no-no. It may cause the plant to "remain stunted and produce only a few small, poor-quality fruits" (Johnny's).

You're more than ready to kick these plants out of the house, but it's still too soon. They're not yet strong enough for life in the great outdoors.

HARDENING OFF

Hardening off is the process whereby you accustom the delicate seedlings to outdoor life by taking them outside on little excursions, like sending the kids to summer camp to get them used to living away from home.

Does this mean packing up all those awkward tippy pots and flats and bringing them outside for a few hours every day, and then bringing them all back inside before dark, and doing this every day for *weeks?*

Yes; that's exactly what it means. Furthermore, all the experts are in agreement for once: hardening off is the one part of the seed-to-plant operation where you can't skimp or fudge.

If you have an enclosed porch, you could put the babies out there and open the windows for a few hours each day. Or you could put them in a cold frame and open and close the vents when appropriate. Or you could tell yourself that hauling plants in and out of the house is good exercise, building the muscles you'll need for the summer's gardening efforts.

"On a mild day, about a week or so before you plan to place a specific transplant out into the garden, begin taking it outside to a protected place (near a wall, for instance) for increasing lengths of time each day, so that it can gradually adjust to conditions outside— a process known as hardening off."

Scott Meyer, in
Organic Gardening,
February 1995

75

GRADUATION

At last the time has come: the plants are ready and the soil is ready. For some plants this moment comes earlier; the leeks can be taken from their pots and put in the ground as soon as the soil is workable, which in my climate means mid-April. With tropical plants like peppers and tomatoes you have to wait until not only is there no longer the remotest possibility of frost, but the soil is actually warm; some years this isn't until mid-June.

The final transplanting is another tricky procedure. Plants that looked large and vigorous growing in pots can suddenly seem frighteningly weak and vulnerable when you wrench them out of those pots and stick them in the ground. In the light of day (hopefully an overcast or cloudy day) they look so puny. Tragedies occur: plants are trampled inadvertently, or they come out of the pot sans roots. Most of them show their unhappiness by getting a serious case of the wilts. Turn the hose on them to revive them and the water knocks them over, washing the soil away from their roots.

It's hard to walk away and leave your baby plants out there unprotected in the cruel world, knowing all the dangers that await them: the cutworms that even now are wriggling into position; the woodchuck pacing just outside the periphery of the garden; the crows circling overhead; not to mention all the blights and rots and funguses lurking in the soil. It's hard to do, but it must be done. Say goodbye and walk away, back to your empty nest: the seedlings are on their own now.

GOURMET GARDENERS

'm a good cook and no doubt you're a good cook, but there are a lot of gardeners out there for whom growing vegetables is an occasion for creating horrid concoctions, about which the best that can be said is that they use up all the Brussels sprouts.

Everyone knows someone like this: he or she clips recipes from gardening magazines (this is equivalent to gleaning medical advice from *Vanity Fair,* or personal grooming tips from *The Atlantic Monthly*), then pulls out the file looking for ideas to adapt to fit the current harvest.

Here's a recipe for a vegetable ragout that uses spinach and peas: sounds good. But the dish also calls for potatoes and they haven't come in yet; let's use turnips instead. Oregano can take the place of tarragon, parsnips for carrots: how about some beets? The result: a Frankenstein's monster of a dish that will then be served to long-suffering loved ones, who will eat every scrap of it and praise it no matter how bad it tastes, because it is *home-grown.*

Even worse than the recipe-victims are those gardener cooks who Invent. They seem to think that because they've successfully grown a few tomatoes and rutabagas, they're automatically endowed with the knowledge of what to do with them; and if all else fails, some hot chili peppers will rescue the meal. Herb-growing is responsible for some of the worst abuses. Since herbs—if they grow at all—produce copiously, the gourmet gardener applies them with a heavy hand: why use a pinch of thyme when entire bushes are to be had? Then there are those funny-tasting herbs (pineapple sage and cinnamon basil come to mind, cross-dressers of the herbary): so easy to grow and so hard to find a use for. Why not throw a few leaves into the pot?

Herbs and vegetables are tossed merrily together—having made only the briefest visit to the sink beforehand—then stirred a few times and *voilà*: garden goulash. "It doesn't get much fresher than this," crows the proud chef as she dishes it up.

The resulting meal is virtuously devoid of butter or olive oil or salt, or any store-bought condiment that might rescue it from dire awfulness. As the guests pick their way through raw chunks of broccoli and slimy overdone zucchini slices, they may encounter the occasional non-food particle: grit? grasshopper leg? it couldn't be a slug, could it? "This is really, uh, fresh," they mutter.

The truth is, the practice of gardening is inimical to good cooking. By the time the gardening day is over, the gardener is too tired to cook. Unable to market, one is forced to make do with whatever is lying about, even if it includes huge zucchinis, wooden beets and over-the-hill potatoes. The longer I garden, the more I find myself tempted into this sort of crime: to turn that huge crop of Swiss chard into a casserole or a pasta sauce; to cook up a unique creation that will, at one and the same time, empty the larder of all that redundant produce and earn me a place in the ranks of the gourmet gardeners.

TO MOW OR NOT TO MOW

Like it or not, what you do with the land around your house tells the world what sort of citizen you are.

A smooth, green, weed-free lawn says that you're a neat, tidy person, with nothing to hide; affluent enough to hire someone to mow the grass or leisured enough to do it yourself. You're someone who might leave his golf course-like estate to play a few rounds of golf on the similarly green grounds of the local country club.

To an environmentalist, though, that carefully nurtured greensward is an ongoing ecological crime, and its owner—*you*—an enemy of the planet, a villain. The green lawn is anti-Green.

Next to having a nuclear power plant in your front yard, having a lawn is about as environmentally incorrect as you can get these days. Immense quantities of noxious chemicals are employed to keep lawns thriving. In addition to the four horsemen—pesticides, fertilizers, herbicides and petrochemicals—they use inordinate amounts of that increasingly endangered resource, water. Even the seed is suspect, since lawn grasses are almost entirely nonnative. And the amount of money spent on lawn care is, needless to say, prodigious: billions of dollars annually.

THE GARDENER'S GRIPE BOOK

"Mowing the lawn, I felt like I was battling the earth rather than working it; each week it sent forth a green army and each week I beat it. . . . I spent part of one afternoon trying to decide who, in the absurdist drama of lawn mowing, was Sisyphus. Me? The case could certainly be made. Or was it the grass, pushing up through the soil every week, one layer of cells at a time, only to be cut down and then, perversely, encouraged (with lime, fertilizer, etc.) to start the whole doomed process over again?"

Michael Pollan
Second Nature

Constant mowing is needed to maintain these green monsters. Hardly anyone has a good word for this exercise; it is boring, it is endless. "Continual amputation," as Sara Stein calls it. Or for the machines: "the angry roar, the horrid fumes" (Eleanor Perenyi); "ought to be outlawed along with chain saws and other noisemakers" (Henry Mitchell).

Greedy and thuggish, lawns impoverish the soil. Their shallow roots form an impenetrable mat, beneath which the earth bakes hard and barren. No flora means no fauna—no robins in spring, no bees or butterflies, no frogs or toads or snakes. (As environmentalists, it goes without saying that we cherish snakes.)

To read current gardening books and magazines you'd think no one has lawns anymore. In *The New York Times,* under the heading "Spring Chores," Anne Raver suggests: "If the lawn needs reseeding, tear it up and plant vegetables." (Easy for her to say.)

Yet a short drive through any suburb or small town quickly reveals that the great American lawn is alive and, if not healthy, certainly no endangered species. And the lawn-care section of the hardware store isn't getting any smaller, either. Even in desert states, homeowners labor away with sprinklers and mow-

80

ers to create the obligatory emerald sward, and where actual grass will not survive they plant substitutes that mimic the real thing (until you test it with a bare foot). Arizona—once a haven for hay fever sufferers—now has as much pollen as the rest of the country, thanks to the lawn cult.

In fact, in some communities keeping one's grass trimmed and verdant is quite literally a civic duty. At least once a year a story hits the press of some rebellious home owner who chooses to plant vegetables or wildflowers or—worst sin of all—nothing in his or her front yard, and runs afoul of the local zoning laws.

Mostly, though, Americans love their lawns. To the settlers who first came to North America, faced with a vast untamed wilderness, a cropped grass lawn must have seemed like the ultimate paradigm of civilization.

According to scientists, our basic genetic coding is what drives us to surround our houses with turf. Humans evolved on the African savannas over a period of two million years, in a landscape of grassy plains dotted with trees: not unlike a fine park. When we mow our lawns, we're trying to re-create those happy long-ago days, dodging lions on the savanna.

"A smooth, closely shaven surface of grass is by far the most essential element of beauty on the grounds of a suburban house. Dwellings, all the rooms of which may be filled with elegant furniture, but with rough uncarpeted floors, are no more incongruous, or in ruder taste, than the shrub and tree and flower-sprinkled yards of most home-grounds, where shrubs and flowers mingle in confusion with tall grass, or ill-defined borders of cultivated ground."

Frank J. Scott, *in* The Art of Beautifying Suburban Home Grounds, *1870*

More immediately, our lawns—like so much of our horticultural baggage—come to us from Great Britain. Rather than model our gardens after the Spanish (who use paving for the flat spaces) or Chinese gardens (which have no flat spaces), we follow the English pattern.

Britain's climate is perfectly suited to lawn-growing. Summers never get as hot or as dry there as they do almost everywhere on this continent. It's the latitude: England being farther north, the grass doesn't fry in the summer as it does in most of the United States. (Of course, the hotter it gets here, the more one craves a cool verdant carpet to wriggle one's toes in.)

The original English lawns were cropped by sheep

"For some time now I've been increasingly convinced that the world would be a better place for gardeners if Edwin Budding and Justus Liebig, two nineteenth-century gentlemen with bright ideas, hadn't let these ideas loose in public. Budding, an English engineer, invented the lawnmower, a device to keep grass short. Liebig, a German professor of science, invented chemical fertilizer, a means to make it grow faster."

Allen Lacy
Home Ground

or, in the case of wealthy landholdings, by me-nials wielding scythes. Then in 1832 a textile engineer with the fertile name of Edwin Budding had a brainstorm: why not adapt the machines used for cutting the pile on carpeting to cut grass? Eureka, the reel mower. The first ones were large, noisy and cumbersome, but they caught on. In the 1890s steam-powered machines were introduced; in 1902, gasoline, and eventually the rotary blade. (Lawn purists insist that only a reel mower does a proper job.) Nowadays the large, noisy and cumbersome ride-on mower is the most popular machine in the United States.

Americans who visit England grow faint with envy at the smoothness, greenness and weedlessness of the lawns. "Rolling" is supposedly the key—hundreds and hundreds of years of peasants pushing large weighty rollers back and forth on the sod, to achieve that flawless surface.

On the other hand, the English practice of cutting lawns in stripes looks really odd to an American eye, accustomed to a seamless sward. Those stripes are highly regarded and are achieved by using either an old-fashioned non-motorized reel mower or—this is so English—a rotary machine that makes stripes as *if* it

"Reel mowers evoke nostalgia: for lost summer mornings when one was awakened by the gentle crescendo and diminuendo of their whirring blades, and the perfume of new-mown grass drifted through an open window. . . . Reel mowers clip like fine scissors, rotary mowers more like a saw slashing at the grass and savagely wounding it—good enough if you are reclaiming a piece of prairie and the last thing you need for a domestic lawn.

An English sward is flat as a billiard table, striped like moire silk, green as an emerald, and apparently weedless."

Eleanor Perenyi
Green Thoughts

83

were an old-fashioned reel mower. I have an idea about those stripes: it has to do with floor covering. In England what we call wall-to-wall carpet (they call it "fitted") is sold in strips that are placed close together, causing a striped effect like an English lawn. In America carpet is sold by the roll; it is laid down in one piece, with no visible seams, like an American lawn. The question is: is the lawn mimicking the carpet, or is it the other way around?

IF NOT A LAWN, THEN WHAT?

Suppose you decide you don't want to get into the lawn rat race. There are several alternatives to grass, some—like paving the front yard with cement and painting it green—less appealing than others. The first that comes to mind is

GROUND COVER. The old standbys—ivy, pachysandra, periwinkle, juniper, etc.—are useful, especially in shady or steep spots where grass won't grow. But here's what you have to do to establish them: the soil must be cultivated "deeper than for bedding plants" (*Wise Garden Encyclopedia*). The plants (which are not cheap) must be individually planted, say eight inches apart, and then watered and *hand-weeded* until they spread to fill the spaces

"Ground covers are useful plants in their place, but one should be wary of any catalogue that promises that a ground cover will grow vigorously in any kind of soil, in sun or in shade, with no assistance from the gardener. There is another word for a plant like that: weed."

Cass Peterson, in
The New York Times,
November 29, 1992

in between; this will take at least a year, probably longer. (You really learn to appreciate the tenacity of grass when it becomes a weed in a juniper bed.) It's a daunting prospect for any but the smallest yard. And you can't ever walk on the plants—not that you'd want to.

If there is an ideal non-grass ground cover, I've yet to hear of it. A recent article in *Organic Gardening* by Lon Rombough lists "34 NON-GRASS GROUND COVERS!" some of which can allegedly be walked upon; a promising number that quickly disappoints. How on earth did lamb's ears, with two-foot-tall flower stalks, get on this list? Or yarrow, with stems so tough they can be used as stakes? Why would anyone want to walk on strawberries, raspberries or cranberries?

Dichondra is also on *OG*'s list of alternative ground covers: a drought-hardy "low-growing plant with round, slightly cupped leaves . . . surprisingly uniform and it needs less mowing than grass." On the down side, it's only hardy to zone 8, which leaves most of us out in the cold dichondra-wise. And "it looks strange," and: "I learned the hard way not to go barefoot in it; parasol-shaped leaves hide insects and slugs."

> "[English ivy] may be a fine plant for large parks, but it is a Trojan horse in a garden. . . . It seems delicate at first, almost frail, but this belief in the innocence of ivy is a cruel delusion. It is entirely tenacious of life, once it gets up steam. Most gardeners I know who plant it eventually regret the decision as they spend weeks ripping it out, often suffering prolonged, painful tendonitis and neuralgia from trying to dislodge the roots from their subterranean havens."
>
> Allen Lacy
> Gardening with Groundcovers and Vines

Chamomile is often recommended as a walk-on grass substitute, and not just by *Organic Gardening*; in England there's a long tradition of camomile (the Brits spell it without the "h") lawns, and a charming novel of that name by Mary Wesley. *OG* offers one caveat: "this is not a good choice for the ragweed allergic; such people could have a reaction to this ragweed relative as well." Chamomile tea is so soporific, I would worry that a lawn of the stuff would send everyone off to dreamland, like the poppy field in *The Wizard of Oz*.

A MEADOW. The trendiest lawn substitute these days is the meadow—or prairie, as some native plant enthusiasts prefer to call it. It turns out, though, that a meadow, which seems like the simplest, most natural thing in the world, isn't easily achieved. If you just stop mowing and let the grass grow, you will not get a meadow; what you'll get after several generations of weeds and brambles, is a forest. Meadows take *work.*

There are "Meadow in a Can" seed mixes that are widely sold, under a picture of a lush planting of colorful wildflowers and gracefully nodding grasses, often with a few butterflies in attendance. Sometimes these mixes are tailored to a particular state or area of the country. The theory is that you stand in your field on a spring day and cast the seeds about you, and before long your field looks just like the picture.

It won't work. You would do as well to skip buying the seeds and simply tear your money into little pieces and scatter it into the wind.

Wildflower seeds need the same sort of attention that any other seed does—sometimes more. The ground must be cleared of any competing plants and cultivated, the seeds have to be planted at the appropriate depth, and watered and weeded until they are established. And even then the meadow of your dreams may not last.

There's a property near us that we drive past often. A few years ago the owners attempted to convert their yard to a meadow. They must have done a good job of preparing the ground, because everything they planted came up and, for the first summer, it was a glorious, envy-provoking spectacle. Poppies, cosmos, bachelor's buttons, daisies, asters and various attractive grasses bloomed until frost; it looked a lot like those pictures. As we drove past it, my husband would say, "We could do that"—thinking of a certain neglected field on our property—and I would say, "Maybe . . ." I was dubious.

The second summer, except for a few poppies there were no more annuals in our neighbors' "meadow." It still looked pretty, though, with tall grass dotted with coreopsis, gaillardia, black-eyed Susans and the usual daisies. The following year there was less color; daisies and Queen Anne's lace were the only flowers that showed up in the now extremely tall grass. That was the summer of the bad drought, and midway through July all the plants in the meadow died; on their feet, as it were, the petrified flowers and grasses standing there, stiff and brown. Not only was it really ugly, but—and this was the clincher for me—it looked *worse* than the untidy roadside verges and neglected fields in the surrounding countryside.

I still want a meadow, someday, when I can figure out how to do it. I know it's important to mow it occasionally—this is probably where my neighbors went wrong—but when? And how often?

At a lecture I attended at the New York Horticultural Society, Sara Stein said that she mows her meadow on the first of May: her garden is south of me, in zone 6. Then I visited Lynden Miller's Connecticut garden, on the cusp of zones 5 and 6, on a garden tour. Miller is a famed landscape designer, creator of the perennial borders in New York City's Bryant Park, among others. Not the least of the wonders of her own gardens was a handsome meadow of grasses and Queen Anne's lace. Her method, she told us, was to cut it to exactly eight inches high on June 15 every year.

Then I came across a photo in *Principles of Gardening* by Hugh Johnson of a truly luscious spring meadow, with wildflowers and bulbs in a tapestry of green grass; it needed only a white unicorn to complete the effect. The caption read: "The grass is only cut three times a year, in late July when the flowers have seeded, late August and November to produce short turf as a setting for spring bulbs." Mowing three times a year is a long way from the concept of a low-maintenance meadow; in fact, cutting an overgrown meadow three times yearly is probably *more* work than trimming a grass lawn every week. Anyway, this enchanting garden is in England, and what works there seldom works here.

Meanwhile my field remains a field: an acre or so of mangy grass and weeds with a few nondescript wildflowers. We have it mowed at varying times with varying results; one year we cut it early in June, and then came the drought. Nothing grew all summer; we looked at a field of ugly brown stubble until September. Happily, this field is far enough away that we don't *have* to look at it all the time. This is not an experiment one would want to conduct outside the front door.

A COTTAGE GARDEN. Rosalind Creasy is a California gardener-writer. Her neighbors were alarmed when she first tore up her front lawn to plant marigolds and eggplants, but over the years they've learned to enjoy the changing displays; wheat one year (she threshed it on the driveway), beans the next. She grows vegetables and flowers everywhere on her small property, redoing the entire planting a couple of times a year.

In nineteenth-century America, instead of lawns people would often have small fenced flower gardens in front of their houses. In a memoir, my mother wrote of hearing that in the 1860s, on her great-grandparents' Maine farm, "there was a big flower garden surrounded by a white picket fence that filled our front yard all the way to the road. Neighbors and strangers would stop to admire the display, and to beg slips for their own gardens." My grandfather, a little boy at the time, had the hated job of weeding and grooming these flowers; as soon as he inherited the property, he plowed the garden under and planted maple trees. (Nowadays that same yard is given over to a grass lawn, with, as its centerpiece, a satellite dish in a ring of geraniums.)

Old-fashioned front yard gardens still exist here and there— Creasy's California experiments belong in this tradition—but they are rare. Like Grandpa, most people don't relish the intense maintenance needed to keep such a public display at the peak of perfection.

A NON-LAWN. What if you had grass but *didn't* use chemicals? What if you got someone else to cut it? What you'd have could

"Old New England villages and small towns and well-kept New England farms had universally a simple and pleasing form of garden called the front door-yard. . . .

When the fences disappeared with the night rambles of the cows, the front yards gradually changed character; the tender blooms vanished, but the tall shrubs and the Peonies and Flowers de Luce sturdily grew and blossomed, save where that dreary destroyer of a garden crept in— the desire for a lawn. The result was then a meagre expanse of poorly kept grass, with no variety, color, or change— neither lawn nor front yard. . . ."

Alice Morse Earle,
Old-Time Gardens,
1901

be called a low-maintenance non-lawn.

My house is surrounded on three sides by non-lawn: a mixture of grass, low-lying weeds, moss and bare spots. When my husband and I bought the property, it came with a riding mower and a push mower, and a person named Roy who runs the machines and takes them to the shop when they act up. Roy is older than us—in this community lawns are cut by retired men—and he has a laissez-faire philosophy about lawn care, which I have adopted.

We never water the grass, unless we're trying to start new seed. We certainly don't feed it; that would only make it grow faster. No pesticides, no herbicides—I walk barefoot in this stuff, I don't want my feet to fall off. The only real weeding I ever do is to pull up those vicious thistles when I can get at them, because they are so painful to walk on.

Roy leaves the clippings on the lawn; they don't add to its appearance, but they presumably decompose and do good things to the soil. (This is one of those hot garden-world controversies: neat freaks vacuum up clippings, claiming they are bad for the grass; lazy folk leave them and say they improve the soil. Take your pick.)

Roy cuts the grass once a week. Sometimes it doesn't all get cut the same day. He likes to do jobs piecemeal; when he gets tired of cutting our grass, he goes down the road and works for one of his other people. This keeps him healthy and accounts for his amazing energy and endurance, not to mention his good humor—although it sometimes makes for a patchy-looking lawn. I find that the best way to look at it is to take your glasses off and sort of scrinch your eyes up. Anyway, it'll all be brown by August.

This scruffy carpet would never pass muster in suburbia— although the very presence of all this turf, and that petroleum-guzzling machine in the barn, automatically disqualifies us as Greens. So be it.

Two Cheers for Grass

Not only am I not about to rip up my lawn and put in a meadow or a vegetable plot; a few years ago I ripped out various gardens to put in a lawn.

The land behind our house slopes up, over gently rising pasture to a hilltop perhaps a half-mile away; this is our view. When we bought the house, the backyard was so cluttered with gardens— a large, sloppy perennial bed; above it a big vegetable garden, full of weed-choked clumps of asparagus; sprawling beds of raspberries and rhubarb—that you really couldn't see the view. Even at its best, in June, when the peonies were in bloom and the vegetable beds newly planted and not yet decimated by woodchucks, it looked like hell.

I puzzled over the problem for almost a year. What to do with the plants? How to open up the view? I studied the site, measured, sketched. A rock garden? There were eight peony clumps, each as big around as my arms; not rock garden material.

My friend Gloria told me to get rid of the plants and put in a lawn, but I hesitated. It seemed wrong to sacrifice peonies and daylilys and asparagus for something as morally bankrupt as a lawn, and yet . . .

One day the man with the bulldozer came to do some necessary earth-moving for us—that gently rising slope was draining into our basement—and I had him dig up everything: perennials, raspberries, asparagus plants. The next day we planted grass seed.

(Bulldozing is wonderful. There is nothing in life that gives as much satisfaction as telling a man to put a hill here, dig up a tree there. It happens so fast! You feel like God Herself.)

We didn't have to sacrifice the various plants after all. The man with the bulldozer dug holes for the peonies, then scooped them up and plunked them into their new homes. This was in April; they were just poking up out of the ground when we moved them and they never missed a beat, flowering six weeks later.

We also moved the raspberries, which needed dividing anyway, and we dug up the asparagus and gave it a new bed. This was done by hand and it was *not easy*. A couple of asparagus plants got left behind, and now every spring we have asparagus spears springing up in the lawn. Roy mows around them—they grow faster than the grass—so that every day or so I can run up the hill and pick a spear or two from the lawn. As for the rhubarb, I'd like to get rid of it—the leaves are poisonous and the rest of it is, well, rhubarb—but neither bulldozers, woodchucks, mowers nor drought seem to affect it.

"Nothing is more pleasant to the eye than green grass finely shorn": so said Francis Bacon (1561–1626). I wouldn't go that far—not in regard to my own clipping-strewn non-lawn—but Bacon definitely was onto something. Grass is *nice.* You can walk on it, you can play games on it, you can have weddings on it. Have you ever heard of anyone getting married on pachysandra?

If you don't go nuts with chemicals, grass is actually pretty cheap. Even the fanciest grass seed mix is affordable, and once the ground is prepared, seeding a new lawn is child's play. (Preparing the ground is *not* child's play, however.) The easiest way to make a lawn, if you're not fussy about its appearance, is to just keep

*... and with turfes
new
Fresh turned, wherof
the grene gras
So small, so thick,
so short, so fresh
of hew
That most like unto
green wool wot I
it was ...*

"The Flower
and the Leafe,"
c. 1400

cutting the weeds short. The quickest—and costliest—method is to buy rolls of sod. You lay it like floor tile, on smoothed tilled ground, and then water like mad. I've done this—it is actually fun, as opposed to, say, planting rosebushes. Sod costs about $2.50 per square foot. What other living plant can cover a square foot of ground for less money?

Grass is cool and makes the air smell sweet. It doesn't distract the eye from a distant view. It enables you to see snakes before they see you—an advantage that would have appealed to our savanna-dwelling ancestors. Grass has a truly miraculous ability to go dormant during a drought: neither those peonies, nor any ground cover I might have planted, could have stayed alive without watering through our dry summers.

Two cheers for grass!

TREE$

Trees are scary. They're big and expensive, with big expensive problems. Put a lot of them together and you've got a forest, with bears and wolves: a really scary proposition.

Trees in a garden are often awkward, like bears in the living room. They tend to be in the wrong place, but moving them is not like getting a friend to lift one end of the sofa so you can try it out under the window. Cutting down trees is expensive and dangerous, and can lead to enraged tree-lovers storming the property, reciting "Woodman spare that tree" or something by Joyce Kilmer. Trees often fall down all by themselves, which can be dangerous and messy. And speaking of messy, it happens to be October and outside my window the maples are shedding something fierce. Leaf-shedding is expensive for the tree owner and necessitates buying costly, noisy machines such as leaf blowers that move the leaves around the yard, and chippers that make more noise than anything.

On the plus side, yes: trees are pretty; you can climb them; they provide shade in August; and when they're in the right place they can hide the neighbor's swing set from view. Californians

*Woodman, spare
    that tree!
Touch not a single
    bough!
In youth it sheltered
    me,
And I'll protect it
    now.*

George Pope Morris,
    "Woodman, Spare
    That Tree," 1830

are said to love trees so much they hug them. (No one knows how the trees feel about this practice.)

Returning to the minus side, trees produce inordinate amounts of pollen at various times during the year, making some people quite ill. Trees themselves have a distressing tendency to come down with illnesses that are either fatal or expensive, or expensive and fatal. If your peonies come down with something, you can spray them or pull them up and buy new ones. If your elm tree comes down with something—*when* your elm tree comes down with something—you call the tree doctor. He scratches his beard (they are all bearded) and tells you the tree will probably die; if you want to save it, it will cost you so many hundreds of dollars for limb-lopping and bandaging and medicating; if you want to give up on it, it will cost just as much to take it down. Naturally, you elect to try to save the poor old dear, which means that this year you pay for the treatment, next year for the removal, unless it lingers on for a few more expensive years, getting cabled and amputated and swabbed with goo until it's so hideous you're not sorry when it finally goes.

If a small tree is in need of help, you'll

probably try to deal with it yourself, at least at first. Garden books give pruning instructions that seem like simplicity itself: remove suckers and water sprouts, open up the center, eliminate crossing branches; and be sure to cut to an outward facing bud, and so on. And here's a diagram showing how it all works. But somehow, out in the open, the tree doesn't look the least bit like the picture. For one thing, the tree is three-dimensional; also, while the one in the picture only has a few well-defined branches, the actual tree has thousands. Those neat cuts in the diagram aren't easy to make, either: the wind blows and the saw slips, and the branch tears. Every cut makes matters worse, and before you know it you've dealt the poor thing a mortal injury.

"There are too many trees in Washington gardens, probably because Americans are brainwashed in elementary school with the notion that trees are sacred. They are not. Trees are, obviously, glorious creatures in their place, but then so are tigers, and we do not insist that every garden have six tigers in it."

Henry Mitchell
One Man's Garden

NEEDY APPLE TREES

Apple trees are the worst. Because they are small, you are tempted to try to doctor them yourself. Up close they turn out to be full of bugs and crawly things, some of them secreting sticky substances. Many of the leaves are damaged or spotted: how are you to know if it's a serious problem or just a passing phase? Just as the diagram in the book bears no resemblance to the actual tree, the bugs won't match the ones on the printed page, either.

Worrying about apple trees is one reason why I sleep poorly these days. All but the purest and greenest organic gardeners find it necessary to spray apples and other fruit trees preemptively; once the ick is on the apple, it may be too late. They're as bad as roses, to which they are closely related. They seem to need year-round attention: dormant oil in the fall, after the leaves drop (but quick, before it gets *too* cold), then a different kind of oil in the spring, then something else when the flowers bloom. At any given moment, there's something I'm not doing for my apple trees. It's like having a very needy relative. You remembered to call on her birthday, but now it's Valentine's Day and you haven't done anything for her.

Still, I wouldn't be without them. Not having apple trees would be un-American. I can't say the same of some of the other trees around here.

LOUSY NORWEGIANS

When my husband and I first looked at the property we now own, it was winter. The front yard was full of great big leafless trees, and there was a little wooden sign over the door that said "Oak House." It did not seem unreasonable to assume that the big trees were oaks.

I love oak trees—they have a wonderful shape, at once massive and graceful. The leaves are shapely, too, and they turn a gorgeous deep red in the fall. (Landscape people and neat freaks dislike oaks because, instead of dropping all their leaves at once, they hang on to them through the winter, scattering a bushel or so at every breath of wind. But I didn't know this at the time.) There's all sorts of lore attached to oak trees, most of it benign, although I suppose the druids did nasty things under them. Anyway, I was glad to have oaks.

Come spring, the trees made leaves; and lo and behold: they were maples, not oaks. There is nary an oak tree on the property. The sign—which we took down—is a mystery. Was it there to trap potential druids? Does it describe the kitchen cabinets? Or does the sign simply describe the wood it is made out of, self-referentially? I use it as a chopping board.

Worse yet, the trees not only weren't oaks, they were Norway maples, or, as Henry Mitchell calls them, "lousy Norway maples." Everyone hates these trees. Garden snobs hate them because they are common as crabgrass; native plant people hate them because they are aliens; and everyone else hates them because they are no good. They're poor team players; they make a blanket of shade that is so black scarcely anything will grow under it, except weeds. The roots gobble up the ground for a phenomenal distance, making a dry, hard compacted surface. Ultimately this affects the health of the tree itself, making it subject to disease; not a fatal disease, just a messy expensive one.

As our eight enormous Norway maples leafed out, we began to wonder what to do about them. The first thought—cut them down, replace them with something better—would have cost as much as buying another house. Then, as the weather grew hot, we realized the shade they gave was not such a bad thing. If only they'd been a little farther away! We needed more privacy, but the maples with their high canopies were useless at shielding the property from the road.

$$$$$$$$$

While we were deciding what to do about the lousy maples—
and it didn't help that some of our friends began to scream
and cry at the very idea of cutting down a tree, while others said,
grandly, "Get rid of them all"—we went to a tree nursery in Massachusetts one day to look for things to plant along the edge of the
lawn as a screen.

Major shock. Trees cost serious money. Shrubs—munchkins of
treedom—also cost. Evergreen shrubs—which was what I needed—
cost even more. (What's the difference between trees and shrubs?
Shrubs are bushy. In fact, shrubs are bushes.) After spending the
equivalent of first-class airfare for two to Paris, we drove away with
a pickup truckload of wee shrubs that looked littler and littler the
closer we got to home. Driving through Great Barrington, down
avenues of hundred-foot-tall spruces, I felt as though I were in the
Emerald City. If a one-foot-by-three-foot hemlock cost fifty dollars,
those spruces must be worth—millions?

That first trip to the nursery was one of those mistakes you learn
from. This was before I fully understood what Norway maples do to
their neighbors. In the parched, shady soil of the front lawn, our new
baby trees were sitting ducks for any passing blight. The magnolia
stellata: dead of scale. The "bargain" river birch: dead of all the numerous diseases birches die from. I managed to rescue the hemlocks before
they too expired, moving them to a wooded area behind the house.
They're growing well, unaware that doom, in the shape of the dread
hemlock woolly adelgid, is advancing inexorably in the Northeast.

The year after my costly educational experience, I bit the bullet and paid a landscaper to put in a hundred-foot hedge of arbor vitae (a sturdy native evergreen that looks like juniper) to edge the lawn. This cost the equivalent of round-trip first-class airfare to China: the front yard owes me big time. The hedge—knock on tree trunk—has thrived so far, a safe distance from the blood-thirsty Norwegians, which are now reduced in number from eight to six.

Having the two maples chopped down was traumatic—for us, at least. We were sure some enraged tree hugger would perform a citizen's arrest. But the only person to notice what we'd done was a neighbor who said he'd been telling the former owners for years that the trees needed to be thinned. Once they were gone, it truly was as though they had never been there—thanks to a cunning little gadget called a stump-grinder, which chomped noisily on the remains until they were reduced to sawdust. We figured out, by counting the rings, that our maples —which we'd assumed were prehistoric or at least pre-Columbian—were a mere forty years old.

TOWERING SPRUCES

I need to plant a couple of trees here and there, for the usual reasons: to provide habitat for birds and other wild critters; to forge a link with as yet unborn generations; to hide a satellite dish. I hesitate, though, afraid of what I might be getting into.

Those hundred-foot-tall spruces on the road to Great Barrington

*I think that I shall
never see
A poem lovely as a
tree.*

. . .

*Poems are made by
fools like me,
But only God can
make a tree.*

*Joyce Kilmer,
"Trees," 1914*

were tiny seedlings once, and not that long ago. They were probably planted in the 1920s.

Picture it: at first a cute little thing in a pot, no bigger than a geranium. You put it next to the front door and give it love and water and fertilizer. In five years it's as tall as you are; at Christmas you string lights on it. In fifteen years it's nudging the roofline. It's beautiful, a thing to be proud of. If it gets too big, you tell yourself you'll cut it down. Forty years go by; now it's forty feet tall. The house is beginning to feel dark, the roof is rotting. Nothing else grows in the yard. But the tree is just getting started. Another thirty years and the house looks like a mailbox. But the tree is magnificent. You—or whoever owns it now—wouldn't dream of taking it down; it would be like killing a loved one. (It would also cost a pretty penny.) Even if you and your spouse agree that the tall beast has outlived its usefulness, the community will never let you chop it down. Airplanes navigate by it! Your only hope is that the people who scout for the White House Christmas tree will spot it and make you an offer. When the neighbors ask, "Whatever happened to that wonderful tree?" you'll say:

"The President wanted it. We had to sacrifice it for the good of the country."

RAINY-DAY PROJECTS

As if there weren't enough to do out in the garden, the experts would now have us bring the garden indoors, to the kitchen. They want us to fill our kitchens with dirt, worms, compost, weeds, bugs and noxious potions.

In addition to cooking *from* the garden, there's no end of cooking to be done *for* the garden: current books and magazines are full of recipes for dubious concoctions, to be whipped up in the blender or microwave. Instead of buying fertilizer, say, or insect repellent, we're encouraged to manufacture our own. In fact, today's gardener-homesteader may find he needs a spare kitchen just for the garden.

These recipes have, I find, two things in common: every single one of them claims to be "easy"—even the ones that are several pages long—and they are, frequently, disgusting. Perhaps these ideas are dreamed up by people who got into gardening because they enjoy the mucking-about-in-the-goo side of the operation; folks who didn't get to play in the mud as kids. For those of us who'd just as soon leave the muck outdoors, it can take a strong stomach to read some of these suggestions.

"I can't believe that the catalogues are now all touting dandelion greens (which I love but they quickly grow bitter as summer nears) and purslane (that rubbery stuff that turns to slime if you are gullible enough to believe what you read and think it might taste good)."

Anne Raver, in
The New York Times,
March 13, 1994

WEED CUISINE. If you can't beat 'em, eat 'em. Or, as the title of a recent article by Jim Duke in *Organic Gardening* magazine says: "EAT YOUR WEEDIES!" While the notion of getting rid of weeds by harvesting and eating them doesn't sound exactly like a labor-saving solution, weed-eating may have other benefits.

It seems some of our most hated nuisance plants are, in fact, edible, and packed with vitamins and other good things. Purslane, which is a major pest in my garden, is particularly touted. The taste is supposed to resemble spinach or chard, and it is high in cancer-fighting vitamins C, A and E, as well as *glutathione* ("a common antioxidant compound that can even detoxify some pesticides!") and omega-3 fatty acids, which are said to lower cholesterol. "No crop . . . is better endowed with a richer variety of health-protecting compounds" (*Organic Gardening*). It is said to have been Gandhi's favorite food. I have used young purslane leaves in salad; it's pleasant-tasting and has a nice crunchy texture. But the word "slimy" is used so often in describing cooked purslane that I think I won't try it.

Stinging nettle has many uses, culinary and medicinal, and it too is high in nutrients. Samuel Pepys enjoyed nettle pudding. Cooked, nettle tastes like spinach. I have eaten it and it was delicious (as might be expected, seeing as the person who cooked it was Paula Wolfert). But the sting of its tiny hairs are so vicious it can be felt through clothing; I wouldn't let nettles into the house.

Lamb's-quarter is yet another spinach analogue. Dr. Duke recommends cooking it with bacon drippings, which would seem to obviate the nutritional benefits. Then there's dandelion, which is actually sold in fancy markets in the spring and can be eaten raw in salad or cooked like escarole; the French like to doll it up with pork *lardons.* Martha Stewart makes wine out of the flowers. But before you rush out to devour your lawn, keep in mind that dandelion is highly diuretic, a fact that is reflected in the plant's French name, *pissenlit*—pee in bed!

Many of our most ubiquitous weeds have long been used medicinally; mullein, burdock, evening primrose and even kudzu are listed as ingredients in remedies sold in health food stores. If you use these potions, you could save yourself a lot of money by, for example, concocting your own evening primrose oil, which is recom-

"If you have limited space, as Ruth Ann Davis does at her mobile home in Tucson, Arizona, try her style of blender composting, which works like a miniature shredder-composter: 'Take kitchen leavings such as carrot tops, melon rinds, and potato peels (but not meat scraps or fibrous, coarse material, like corn cobs) and grind them with a little water in your blender."

Shelley Goldbloom
Garden Smarts

mended for premenstrual syndrome. On the other hand, lots of weeds are toxic to some degree, or in some part of the plant. Rampant experimentation could be fatal: Kids, *don't* try this at home.

KITCHEN COMPOST. Of course you compost every last potato peeling, eggshell, coffee ground and rotten onion. (Of course you do.) And unless you're able to run out to the compost heap every time you have a carrot peeling to dispose of, you probably keep some kind of bag or bucket in the kitchen. Now the garden mavens are suggesting that the entire composting process can take place in that bucket, right in your nice clean kitchen. And not in just any old bucket, either.

To accelerate the process, the manufacturers of the Vita-Mix juicers recommend using their machine to grind up leftovers, including bones and old bread. The resulting "juice" can then either go into the compost pile, or be added directly to plants, with dazzling results. (They do have the delicacy to stipulate that you use separate containers for composting and the stuff you're going to eat.)

Several companies offer special kitchen compost collectors. There's a cute little countertop model in the Plow & Hearth catalog, for $9.95, which looks like a miniature of their big black outdoor bin selling for $89. Gardener's Eden's version is more serious; it's bright green plastic, has a charcoal filter and a handle, and says COMPOST in big letters to warn the unwary ($14.50). Smith & Hawken will sell you a two-gallon galvanized bucket with handle and lid for $34, which seems like a lot for a bucket. All of these containers have airtight lids, which would keep the smell in—until that awful moment when the lid has to be lifted. (Knowing myself, I'd probably throw the thing away after a few weeks, rather than open it.)

If you're really serious about indoor composting, you might want to look into . . .

WORMS (vermiculture, if you want to be fancy). As everyone knows, earthworms—also known as red worms—are grand little garden helpers. They live underground (their very presence is an indicator of soil health), and in their tunnelings and squirmings aerate the soil, adding nutrients to it with their "castings"—the technical name for worm doodoo. Earthworms are hermaphrodites, and the babies come from eggs. Contrary to popular legend, cutting them in half does not create two new worms, although if you cut their heads

"VITA-MIX TURNS GARBAGE INTO ODOR-LESS COMPOST AND FREE FERTILIZER
'. . . Over the past year my wife and I have been composting most of our non-meat kitchen waste by pureeing our garbage in the Vita-Mixer 4000. We then pour the liquid garbage into a composting tumbler loaded with chopped leaves. . . . We keep an extra Vita-Mix container under the kitchen sink, and when it is full (about every 1 or 2 days) we add water and pour it into the compost heap.' "

Advertisement for Vita-Mix

off they can sometimes grow new ones. These experiments are not recommended ways of increasing the worm population; you might just wind up with a lot of cut-up dead worms.

Earthworms have been sold to gardeners (as well as fishermen) for generations; the Gurney's catalog offers them under a picture of a pink comet-shaped worm with a maniacal grin on its face. Nowadays they are even being promoted as house pets. The idea is to keep them in a pail in your kitchen and feed them leftover vegetable matter, which they will then turn into compost.

The Rodale *Encyclopedia of Organic Gardening* explains at length how to do it—a not entirely trouble-free process, it seems to me, reading between the lines. For the bedding, combine "2 parts commercial steer manure, 2 parts sawdust, and 1 part shredded leaves. Garden soil may also be added." You mix it and let it rest for a few days, making sure it doesn't get too hot, before adding your new friends. Drainage, aeration and temperature are all vital, as is the necessity of keeping the bin well covered to keep flies out and smell in. Earthworms won't eat just any old thing. "Soft foods are best for the first few days" (as when adopting a new kitten), and then

"The gardener with soil full of earthworms can bless himself, for they are a sign of good tilth and fertility. But they don't go willingly about their useful work in poor, hard ground where they are most needed. It's another case of them as has, gets."

Eleanor Perenyi
Green Thoughts

they're ready for their regular diet of "oatmeal, peanut hulls, toast, fruit and vegetable trimmings, and coffee grounds."

Another source (Doc and Katy Abraham) informs me that onions must be avoided, as the worms dislike them so much they will *crawl out of the bin* to get away from them. And the food should be pureed (in the Cuisinart?) because "worms don't have teeth to tear off large chunks." If all goes well, after sixty days you should have a bin full of rich compost and a new generation of wrigglers.

If all does not go well, you may, like *New York Times* garden writer Anne Raver, find "brown goo oozing out of the air holes in [her] worm box." Apparently, if they get hungry enough, they will eat first each other, then their castings, and then turn into brown goo. (Brown goo, as the article makes clear, is not a Good Thing.)

One is not very surprised to learn that there are commercial worm bins on the market, designed to take some of the guesswork out of the aerating and odor control factors. The Gardener's Supply Company catalog offers a large green plastic bin; the complete kit, including worms and bedding, will run you over $75. The book, *Worms Eat My Garbage*

"One favorable aspect of having worms as pets is that you can go away without having to make arrangements with the vet. . . . It really is amazing to reach into my worm bin and pull out a handful of rich, sweet soil, wriggling with worms. 'Look!' I say to my friends. 'Later!' they say."

Anne Raver, in
The New York Times,
January 23, 1994

(does Oprah know about these people?), is another $9.95. Smith & Hawken's "Vermi Composter" is black, has an outside tap to release "nutrient-rich compost tea" and sells for $98, worms included.

I haven't yet succumbed to the joys of vermiculture—worms strike me as exactly the sort of thing I want to keep *out* of my kitchen—but I can see where it could be a fun project for a ten-year-old boy; an ant farm for the '90s.

BREW YOUR OWN ORGANIC PEST REPELLENTS. There seems to be no end of these recipes; I've assembled three fairly typical ones.

1. Hand-pick some of the critters you want to repel (such as slugs or Japanese beetles) and put them in the blender with some water. Now turn it on; this is the fun part. You pour the resulting "tea" on the besieged plants, where it presumably sends a strong message to the pest; the bug's equivalent of finding a horse's head on his pillow.

2. Mix up hot peppers with vinegar and garlic to make a sort of repellent salsa. Hot peppers are alleged to drive away all kinds of varmints, from squirrels and insects to cats and dogs. (My experience does not bear this out. One year when I was battling squirrels on my city terrace and I happened to have an excess of chili peppers, I

spread the little chilies liberally in the flower beds. The next day I looked out the window to see squirrels playing with them, tossing the peppers into the air and catching them; when they got bored with the game, they went back to their real job, digging up tulip bulbs.)

3. "Soak one cigarette in a cup of warm water for one day; strain and add a quarter teaspoon olive oil and a quarter teaspoon liquid soap" (*The New York Times*; review of a book called *Kill Bugs Dead,* by Diane Martin). This is supposedly good for repelling aphids; it is certainly repellent. One question: Why olive oil and not, say, safflower? And if it must be olive oil, should it be Extra Virgin, or will any old pressing of the olive do?

STERILIZING SOIL. The notion of sterilizing dirt sounds like a joke, except that people actually do it. It seems that soil from the garden, or soil that has been used for potted plants, may harbor microorganisms that could cause the dread "damping off" disease, thus aborting your infant seedlings before they see the light of day. But buying soil in bags from the store can get costly. Very costly. The solution: sterilize the old stuff by baking it in the oven.

"Spread about a gallon of dirt into a shal-

"The cure for grasshopper invasions is grasshopper puree. Take a couple dozen grasshoppers, medium to large size, alive or dead (preferably fresh), and place in a blender with enough water to thin 'em down. Blend at high speed several minutes. The result can be sprinkled with a watering can onto the plants you wish to protect or strained with a fine sieve and then sprayed on . . ."

Patricia Briney,
letter in Organic
Gardening,
May/June 1994

low baking pan, add a cup of water and bake in a 180-degree oven for 45 minutes," goes one recipe. Another expert suggests cooking your dirt several hours; yet another warns never to cook it longer than half an hour, for fear of killing the good guys along with the villains. One quaint method involves burying a small potato in the pan: when the potato is perfectly cooked, the dirt is ready. I've also read that if the soil is cooked too much there's a danger that toxic elements may be activated or, conversely, that the desirable microorganisms will be killed.

A number of writers mention an unholy aroma that fills the house in the course of this operation; one recommends putting the dirt into those plastic oven bags more commonly used for cooking chickens, to contain the smell. For myself, I'm still buying bags of Jiffy-Mix at the Agway; think of all the money I'm not spending on fuel, plastic oven bags and wasted potatoes!

SMELL

Flower lovers have been complaining for years that scent has vanished from the garden. Put your nose into a modern rose and sniff; most often, nothing at all happens.

The blooms of one's childhood memories were sweetly aromatic; those of today are scentless or, like chrysanthemums and marigolds, slightly nasty. Breeders and hybridizers are usually blamed for this state of affairs: while striving for disease resistance, earliness/hardiness, ruffled/doubled/fringed petals, gigantic flower heads with dwarfed stems, nonstop bloom, unusual colors, etc., fragrance got lost, left off the shopping list.

Recently, though, with the vogue for heirloom and antique plants, scent has become *hot.* Plant and seed catalogs mention fragrance on practically every page, attributing "delicious" or "romantic" or "heavenly" smells, often to plants whose actual aroma may be quite modest. There are entire books on the subject of designing scented gardens, and something called "aromatherapy," which finds medicinal uses for all that fragrance. You just know that somewhere, in some laboratory, scientists are building a rose that smells like Chanel No. Five. Scent sells.

The worst manifestation of this mindless perfume pursuit—to my mind, and to my nose—is those shops that sell potpourri and dried flower wreaths and scented candles, and that cause me to begin to sneeze even before the door chimes have stopped tinkling.

Scent is nice, but enough is enough. A garden in which all the flowers pump clouds of perfume into the air (like those people who ambush you in department stores with scent samples) would be intolerable. Happily, such flowers are rare, even—especially—among heirlooms.

According to rosarian Stephen Scanniello, who runs the Brooklyn Botanic Garden's famed rose garden, "some antique roses really have little scent at all." A few years ago I planted an heirloom rosebush *(Rosa celsiana)* that was described by White Flower Farm as "intensely fragrant." The blooms have a pleasant enough smell, but you really have to bury your face in them to get it.

Most flowers keep their fragrance to themselves, as is proper. A field full of lily-of-the valley will have no smell at all, unless you bruise or cut the blossoms. "Aromatic" herbs mostly aren't; you have to pinch the leaf of a sage plant or a scented geranium to release the scent.

I grow a lot of lavender. In the heat of summer, with bees buzzing madly about the purple flower spikes, the smell can just barely be sensed. It is subtle, more of a feeling than an actual aroma, which is its charm. The reason those egregious potpourri shops stink is that the scents are enhanced with perfume oils.

Then there are the flowers whose fragrance is neither modest nor subtle, flowers that can fill a room with scent—and empty it of people. Last spring I bought a little pot of blue hyacinths; "so sweetly fragrant, it takes only one to perfume an entire room" (Wayside Gardens, Fall 1994 catalog). As the flowers began to open, the scent did indeed perfume the room, at first sweet, then cloying, then unbearable. I put the pot in an unused room, but the smell escaped into the rest of the house; finally I put it out on the porch, where it sandbagged us every time we went out the door. Paperwhite narcissus is another olfactory offender: these plants, ubiquitous at Christmastime, have a sharp, almost medicinal odor that makes you wonder if you've left the gas on. But the catalogs that sell them invariably describe them as "fragrant."

All these judgments are, of course, subjective; even though an informal survey of my friends found no one who actually likes the smell of paperwhites, there is

probably someone somewhere who loves it. In late summer when my Oriental lilies bloom, the heavy perfume fills the garden. I find it thrilling, but my husband wrinkles his nose and says, "What's that smell? Is it one of those magazine inserts?"

Smell is in the nose of the beholder, or to put it another way: My lily is fragrant, yours is aromatic, his stinks.

EPIPHANIES IN THE
HERBACEOUS BORDER

I wasn't going to get into perennials. We were looking for a country property, a quiet, peaceful weekend retreat; it was my shot at tranquillity, and I didn't want to give it up for a bunch of flowering plants.

If I'd learned one thing from twenty years of trying to garden on Fire Island, it was that perennials are Trouble. Expensive to buy and difficult to maintain, they need constant weeding, deadheading and trimming to look their best. Actually they only look their best for that brief moment when they are in flower, and then they go back to looking their worst. Many perennials, I'd concluded, prefer to live in England and show their disdain for this country by dying. Even at home they're chancy: wasn't it an Englishman who said, "A perennial is a plant that, had it not died, would have returned the following year"? Plants that don't give up the ghost the first year often turn out to be weeds—"invasive" is the polite term—running rampant all over the garden.

Those gorgeous flowering borders in the picture books are, I'd decided, unattainable fantasies; something to dream about, like having a Monet over the fireplace. In fact, many houses with such gardens do boast the equivalent of Monets, and this gives you an idea of the financial commitment such a border necessitates.

I did want flowers, though. At the same time that the sensible side of my head was determined not to become enslaved by a flower garden, another part of my brain was dreamily envisioning a fuzzy flower-filled Hallmark Card-like image of our country retreat. (Could this be a case of the right brain not knowing what the left brain is thinking?)

I saw hollyhocks and lavender and peonies, and maybe a couple of rosebushes; irises, of course—along with tulips and daffodils and a few other bulbs (I am half Dutch, after all). A closer look at the picture might reveal foxgloves and delphiniums and poppies and campanula and lupines . . . But I wasn't going to get crazy.

The property we finally settled on, after a six-month search, was an 1830s farmhouse, with ten acres of barns, streams, trees, fields and an "Established Perennial Border." It was winter when we first saw the place, and I didn't give the garden much thought at first.

The closing was delayed until June. Over the course of the spring we visited the property a number of times, and as the border emerged from first snow and then mud I began to take notice of it. It was some ninety feet long, running southeast-northwest, an irregular rectangle between three and nine feet wide. It was surrounded, and in parts overrun, by grass. Between it and the house there was a driveway; paralleling the border on the far side was a wooden fence with a cow pasture beyond it, and the public road curving around the pasture.

When my landscape designer friend Gloria, who has a cold and ruthless eye, came to visit she let me know that my best course would be to root out all the perennials and put in a row of evergreen shrubs. Gloria believes that flowers should be grown in cutting gardens screened from public view, like hospital patients recovering from surgery.

I knew the perennial border might spell the end of my hope of rustic repose, but I couldn't follow Gloria's advice because by this time I had spotted the little red shoots of peony plants pushing up through the soil. In any case, I'm incapable of throwing out plants, even ones I don't like. I decided to keep the border, at least until I had seen it through one full year's bloom.

From time to time during these months, I would pick up one of my old gardening books and leaf through the pages on perennials. Just as I remembered, beside the luscious photos there were pages and pages of text, with diagrams and instructions for dividing and propagating, and lots of technical terms like *cultivar* and *rhizomatous* and *sepal*. Worst of all was the endless fussing about aesthetic issues: complex color harmonies, foliage texture, mass, form, volume. As I put each book away, I'd reconfirm my resolve not to let the perennials drive me crazy.

"There are . . . certain harsh shades of mustard yellow that we shall have to use discreetly. Achillea filipendulina (eupatorium) *'Gold Plate,' for instance. . . . what shall we grow next to our 'Gold Plate'? Shall it be the spires of cobalt-blue delphiniums? Certainly not. The contrast is effective but utterly crude."*

Christopher Lloyd
The Well-Tempered Garden

119

SPRING, YEAR ONE:
AN EPIPHANY

My husband and I were having a celebratory lunch (we'd just signed the mortgage papers) in a New York restaurant, a few weeks before the final closing on the house. Through the window I saw, across the street, one of those sidewalk flower displays outside a Korean green market. There were roses and carnations and lilies and chrysanthemums, all the colors of the spectrum, massed together without concern for what "went" with what. The effect was one of abundance and beauty.

"Look, Don," I said to my spouse. "Orange and blue and purple and yellow, even red, and it's wonderful. That's what I want in my garden." A riot of color—no rules, no discrimination. I'd use the border as a cutting garden, and when I needed elegant color combinations I would create them indoors.

The day before the closing I bought a big ironstone pitcher at a flea market. When we finally got to the house, while Don unpacked, and plugged in lamps and put up window shades, and made the many and often unhappy discoveries of home owning (like the windows being mysteriously glued shut), I picked flowers.

It was the first week of June: there were masses of peonies, in many shades of pink; blue and yellow irises, poppies, daisies, foxgloves, some blue spiky things that later turned out to be veronica, bleeding heart, coralbells, columbine. I crammed them into the ironstone pitcher and they were glorious.

I spent much of that first summer getting acquainted with the perennial border. After the peonies stopped blooming, the garden never again attained the lushness and gay abandon of that first week. There were Problems. The border had been neglected for several years and was full of weeds. The edges were ragged and shapeless, grass and dandelions from the lawn wandered in and out at will.

The flowers appeared to have been stuck in any old way. Tall plants stood in front of short ones. There were gaps where nothing grew but grass, and there were thickets where irises, daisies and monarda slugged it out in hand-to-hand combat. While still determined not to go crazy, I could see there was work to be done.

Many of the plants needed to be "divided"—a procedure I had read about and which filled me with dread. Then one day Roy, who mows our lawn, saw me wrestling with some grass-choked veronica; he plucked it out of the ground with his fork, pulled the roots apart, separating them from the grass, and finally chunked it back into the ground in three healthy pieces. The entire operation took him less than five minutes. When I tried it myself, I realized that upper body strength was the factor that the books had neglected to mention.

Much of my time was taken up with making a map of the border, like the ones in the gardening books—except that my efforts didn't look the least bit like those in the books. It turned out to be extraordinarily difficult to put the border on paper. The fence behind the garden was built in six-foot sections, so I spray-painted numbers, from 1 to 15 on the posts. This gave me at least a framework, although it was still hard to pin things down; the peony that seemed to be in front of 8 from one angle, would be at 7½ from another. (Two years later, when I saw an aerial photo of our property, I discovered that the border was not, in fact, quite parallel to the fence.)

Most of the plants were unfamiliar to me. Every day when I went out to the garden, along with the usual arsenal of tools I packed a notebook and pencil, a yardstick and two books: *Taylor's Guide to Perennials* and the *Golden Guide to Wildflowers of North America.* I spent many hours leafing through these books, comparing the pictures with the actual plants. The moments when I was able to actually identify anything were so rare I would scream with delight—even if the plant turned out to be a noxious weed.

The map I drew was full of guesses and question marks. There was "low hairy spotted, early ppl flwrs"; that turned out to be lungwort (*pulmonaria*). There was "AW"—Attractive Weed—and "FLS"—Floppy Stuff. (We had—and have—acres of it. I still don't know its name.) Looking at this plan five years later, I see a chill-

ingly accurate sketch of a mallow leaf (one of my worst weeds) with the legend "creeps & vines, lav flowers, geranium?"

While I was coddling the dread mallow, I was ripping out handfuls of a low grassy plant that, because there was so much of it, I was convinced must be a pest; it proved to be grape hyacinth (*Muscari*). A forgiving soul, it flourished where I flung it.

The entire south end of the border was choked with tall, weedy-looking plants: "FM"—Formless Mess—was (and still is) the name for this area. Its components were phlox, physostegia, monarda, veronica and wild asters, all intermixed with each other and extremely difficult to tell apart until they flowered: an event that the physostegia and asters put off until the last possible moment.

If I'd had nothing else to do, the perennial border would have been more than I could handle. As it happened, I had a great deal to do that year. We were entirely overhauling the interior of the house—electricians and plumbers and carpenters swarmed over the property. Elsewhere we were dealing with vexing landscaping problems: the fact that all the trees seemed to be in the wrong places, the question of where best to locate the swimming pool, and where to move the vegetable garden.

My husband, meanwhile, had discovered that a peculiar concave rock garden in the front yard had once been an ornamental pond, and he spent many weeks digging it out. As

"I think the secret of your gardening is that you have the courage to abolish ugly or unsuccessful flowers. Except for those beastly red-hot pokers which you have a weakness for, there is not an ugly flower in the place."

Harold Nicolson,
in a letter to Vita
Sackville-West,
1937

123

he dug up plants and bulbs, he threw them into the wheelbarrow. It was my job to replant them someplace before they died, although I had no way of knowing whether they were weeds or plants. Mostly I stuck them into bare spots in the border, just to get them out of the wheelbarrow. One little shrub, which I planted at the north end, seemed for so long to be dead that I named it "DT"— Dead Thing; a year later it came to life and is now known as "FDT," or Former Dead Thing. It seems to be some sort of wild dogwood and—after four years—has yet to flower.

Some days the wheelbarrow was full of irises and daylilies and rosebushes, and I was kept busy running around the property finding spots for them. I began to get a sense of what did and did not belong in the perennial border: the big sprawling daylilies didn't fit in; neither did small dainty plants like pinks. It wasn't always easy to find places for the foundlings; this is one of the sneaky ways a garden engenders more gardens, by making you create homes for its outcasts.

Lily bulbs turned up; I'd never grown actual lilies—as opposed to daylilies—and had always thought them impossibly fragile and finicky. I carefully replanted them, tucking them into the border, and was thrilled a few weeks later to see them shoot up tall flower stalks. I was less than thrilled when, almost without exception, the flowers proved to be orange. "Why orange?" I asked (I had a garden journal now). In a county that is, in July, paved with orange daylilies, why grow orange *lilies*? But I still adhered to my non-discriminatory color policy.

There was much to gripe about in my new flower garden. I kept finding bulbs in the back of the border that logically belonged in front. Clematis was growing on a spindly trellis, in the heart of the "FM" section. I dug it up—armed with a pitchfork and newly found confidence—and put it against a sunny wall of the house, where it has thrived, sharing a border with those long-wished-for hollyhocks, which have not thrived (Rust).

Other problems were less amenable. The length of the border made it hard to get around; if you walked across it, you risked trampling on plants. In many ways, the entire bed was in the wrong place. It was so far from the house you could see it only from the kitchen, although it was in full view of the road. Since the front of the border—the viewing side—faced the tree-shaded west, the flowers didn't get any afternoon sun and consequently leaned away from the viewer. Some of them leaned so far they looked as if they were trying to escape.

There was one tall clump of unknowns that kept getting bigger and bigger. Finally, in August, eight feet tall and wide, it began to bloom: fluffy yellow mum-like flowers. On the map I wrote: "Heliopsis? Sunflower? Helianthus?" (I still don't know which it is; once again, the books were less than helpful. I call them sunflowers.) The plant—or plants—were way out of scale to the rest of the border; they needed to be moved, but where to? Rain made the tops droop down, and I picked huge bouquets of the sodden stems, filling the house and porch with them, giving bunches away to friends, to neighbors, to the woman who delivers the mail. The flowers lasted a week or more indoors, new buds opening every day. Ungainly and out of scale though they were, I realized I couldn't part with the plants. The border was working its wiles on me, seducing me.

That summer I discovered that local garden centers sold healthy potted perennials, for a reasonable price. Following my Riot Of Color aesthetic, I plunked them in wherever I found room, thereby repeating the errors of the previous owner. I made new friends: Jacob's ladder, marguerite, purple coneflower. Delphiniums purchased in July flowered in August.

Criticism gave way to admiration. There wasn't much rain that summer, and I never watered the perennial border, yet the flowers flourished. In my Fire Island garden I used to have to tie stakes to each little plant, even the lowest-growing zinnias. Here even the tallest plants grew strong stalks that needed no support. Digging in the bed I found dark cool cow manure-enriched humus: I realized that with all their mistakes, the previous owners had done a fine job of preparing the soil for my border. One day I realized that I had fallen in love. So much for tranquility; goodbye, rustic repose.

Being in love didn't make the problems go away; if anything, it made them more urgent. The asters: big gawky bushes that didn't do anything except get larger and uglier until the end of the summer, whereupon they produced insignificant little dirty-white daisy-like flowers; a poor reward after such a long wait.

(Though there was one variety of aster that made a handsome bright pink flower, which I was glad to see late in the year. A blowsy plump hausfrau of a plant, it answers to the name *Alma potschke.*) In October I launched a major vendetta, uprooting every hated wild aster.

That winter, as the snow drifted over the brown stalks that were all that remained of my border, I dreamed of next summer's flowers: an image reminiscent of a Hallmark card; full of delphiniums, devoid of asters . . .

Spring was a revelation. Those low spring flowers that I'd censured for being in the back of the border; it turned out they were in the right place after all. In April, before anything else had begun to grow, the six-inch-tall grape hyacinths were a knockout. They were succeeded by all kinds of tulips, including the wild-and-crazy parrots. I bought more delphinium plants, most of the past year's having expired. I puzzled over the emerging aster shoots in the FM; how could there be so many of them? The irises came down with "iris borer." I almost fainted when I stomped on the first white grub, but by the one hundredth I gave it no thought. The peonies were celestial.

Life was good.

YEAR TWO:
THE SECOND EPIPHANY

It all fell apart on July 23rd. I went out to the garden to find a cacophony of warring colors. The delphiniums—a mixture of royal blue, white and pale blue—were shrieking insults at an orange tiger lily, some scarlet monarda, and a clump of sulphur-

"People have a habit of saying airily that 'flower colours never clash!' I should like them to have heard what a certain scarlet geranium of my acquaintance said to a neighbouring fuchsia, last spring. They might then alter their opinion."

Beverley Nichols
Down the
Garden Path

yellow yarrow *(Achillea filipendulina)*. Although I quickly picked the lilies and took them into the house, the noise continued. I pulled up the monarda. (This plant, a pretty enough thing with a nice scent, wanders freely through the garden. It's easy to pull up, but it always pops up again. It's about midway between a nuisance and a welcome guest.)

It was no use; the delphiniums and the yarrow could not co-exist. I was shaken. My Riot Of Color philosophy flew out the window, along with my peace of mind. *Why* didn't they want to get along? I whined. After

all, blue and yellow are supposed to be friends. Did this mean that I had to have a Color Scheme?

I hit the books. I read about hue and value and tone and the color wheel: contrast was good, but then so was harmony; warm colors leap at you, cool ones retreat; white is a mediator, white is a troublemaker; blah blah blah.

I read about Vita Sackville-West's White Garden at Sissinghurst. Gertrude Jekyll's perennial border, I learned, was 200 feet long and 14 feet wide, with the colors graduated—warm reds and yellows in the middle, modulating to soft blues and silvers at the ends. I didn't feel I could carry off something like that, and I wasn't sure I'd even like it. Where would there be a place for serendipitous combinations, like the happy contrast of blue balloon flower (*Platycodon*)—the only thing I had to show after twenty years on Fire Island—and golden yellow coreopsis?

I visited the perennial borders in the Central Park Conservatory Garden and noted that the plan repeated blues, whites and violets, with some yellow, less pink, very little red, and lots of interestingly hued foliage. In magazines I saw plenty of tasteful displays that relied on pastels; you couldn't get into trouble, it seemed, if you kept to blue, lavender and pink. But I loved my yellows too much to give them up.

Blue-and-yellow gardens excited me more; I could live in a world without red or pink, I thought. But then I remembered the peonies. And what would I do with all the phlox?

The problem with the perennials was that I couldn't bear to get rid of any of them. I had to find a way to make them get along with each other.

YEAR THREE:
THE THIRD EPIPHANY

One day—appropriately enough in the third year—the clouds parted and the solution appeared in three parts: Time, Color, Space.

TIME

Here in my corner of zone 5, the flowering season divides into three. The first, spring, begins in late April with the blue-purple lungwort and a few bulbs—grape hyacinth, orange fritillaria, various tulips—and winds up with the explosion of pink peonies and blue and pale yellow irises in June. From beginning to end it is pretty. The bright pure hues of early spring are welcome after the long winter. Then, just as they're beginning to seem a bit much, everything turns pink. You wouldn't want to live with it forever, but for two weeks it's gorgeous—and there are those irises, for relief. The light is soft and the grass is a tender, new green. Spring is no problem.

There's not much of a problem in the fall, either: the violets and purples and mauves (phlox, salvia, autumn sedum, aster, physostegia) harmonize nicely with the lingering golds of chrysanthemum, black-eyed Susan, perennial sunflower and coreopsis, with silvery artemisia to set it all off; the warm autumn light mediating any conflicts that might arise.

Summer is the problem. It's barely two months: from the fading of the peony bloom in June, to late August when the yarrow quits. The flowers of summer are aggressive prima donnas, greedy for attention. "Look at me! Me! Me!" they clamor. The sun shines hot, and the sky is an intense blue that rivals the delphiniums. This is the time when a Color Scheme is desperately needed.

COLOR

I decided to divide my long perennial border into three beds; blue, yellow and pink-purple. It might have been more logical to put the blue in the middle, but I wanted to leave the perennial sunflowers where they were; their size made them a natural center-piece. I didn't want to do any more plant-moving than absolutely necessary.

Keeping a summer-only color policy meant that I didn't have to, for example, dig up eight massive peony clumps and put them in the pink section of the border. By summer, their flowers faded, the peonies' handsome dark green foliage makes a nice background for the summer colors. (By fall that foliage is less at-tractive, but that's another story.) I could and did use my new policy as a rough guide, so that when my neighbor gave me a basketful of yellow irises I relegated them to what would become the Yellow Bed.

"Yellow is a contro-versial colour. People shy away from mauve as a word but are perfectly content to grow the majority of mauve flowers pro-vided they are dis-creetly described as lavender or lilac. With yellow it is the color itself that frightens them. There are many keen gar-deners who have to let you know, as soon as gardens and plants start to be discussed, that they are not prepared to tolerate yellow or orange flowers."

Christopher Lloyd
The Well-Tempered
Garden

"There is nothing more difficult to do in outdoor gardening than to plant a mixed border well, and to keep it in beauty throughout the summer. Every year . . . I find myself tending towards broader and broader effects, both of grouping and colour."

Gertrude Jekyll

The Blue Bed, at the north end, would be the home of the lordly delphiniums. Other blues—campanula, baptisia, Jacob's ladder, platycodon, salvia, Russian sage, caryopteris, any and every blue flower I could lay my hands on (blue is my weakness)—would be tucked in here and there, with coralbells and daisies for soft contrast. By this time I had actually read Gertrude Jekyll (as opposed to reading *about* her famed color-graduated border). Jekyll says that a blue garden should be "beautiful first, and then just as blue as may be consistent with its best possible beauty." Right on! White and pink lilies (the lily is one of the few flowers that can talk back to a delphinium) would gradually replace the orange ones and the yarrow, which would be exiled to . . .

The Yellow Bed, in the center. Coreopsis, marguerites, yellow and gold lilies would join the existing sunflowers. All the yarrow would be massed at the rear of the bed, with artemisia growing through it. Friends of yellow—purple coneflower, poppies—would also find a home here. Yellow turned out to be the easiest to plan and execute; the hardest was . . .

The Pink-Purple Bed, at the south end,

home of the infamous Formless Mess. The colors aren't a problem: there are phloxes in a wide range of pinks, reds and white; magenta physostegia, purple veronica, mauve Joe Pye, pink and mauve lilies, mixed foxgloves and lupines; with monarda allowed to wander about, and pink columbines and coralbells as edging.

The problem is a structural one; no matter what I plant, it instantly gets lost in the jungle of formlessness.

SPACE

When I redid the border, I divided it into three oval beds, each twenty-eight feet long and nine feet wide in the middle, tapering to two feet, with mulched pathways in between, big enough to get the wheelbarrow through. The narrow ends of the beds make nice spots for growing low floppy plants, like my beloved platycodon. Even though I tried to keep the digging and plant-moving to a minimum, it was a *big* job. I hired a strong young man to do the heavy work, which made it an *expensive* job.

In most perennial borders the plants stand in size places: little ones in front, tall ones in back. I can't do this, because this border is vis-

" 'I warned you to use plenty of wisteria lavender and sweet-pea pink,' said an experienced gardener at the time, surveying my dull effect and quite pleased (for gardeners are not angels, let me tell you) to see it had worked out as badly as she had predicted."

Henry Mitchell
The Essential
Earthman

"White is commonly recommended— by the blind, I have often suspected— as a great pacifier of warring colors. I find it eggs the warriors on. . . ."

Henry Mitchell
The Essential
Earthman

ible from all sides, and gets most of its sun from the "back." I haven't yet licked the problem of the afternoon shade. From my point of view it can be a blessing; it's pleasant working in the border in the late afternoon, in the summer (not quite as pleasant as a dip in the pool). But the shade makes the plants lean away from the viewer. "Why are all the flowers turning their backs on us?" my husband once asked.

I try to relegate the really tall plants to the middle of the beds—like a spine running down the center—but things happen. Sometimes plants refuse to stay put. Often they prove to be a different size than advertised: what was supposed to be a towering six-foot lily turns out to be an insignificant little flower, huddled under the peony plants. I'm trying to introduce small shrubs into these center positions, but there too I've had setbacks. The "white" deutzia I put in the Yellow Bed proved to be more pink than white; the purple smokebush looked nice in Pink, icky in Blue. The one in Pink, however, was the one that got sick and died.

I grow lowish, shade-fond plants in the fronts of the beds: coralbells, columbine and bleeding heart in Blue and Pink; alchemilla and Stella d'Oro daylily in Yellow. This has worked pretty well, except that the columbine looks awfully ratty after its spring bloom is finished. I'm thinking of moving it somewhere.

In the back I try for masses of bloom, with mixed success. The physostegia has this job in the Pink Bed, but it blooms so late there isn't much to look at until the end of August. (The physostegia is a pest in a lot of ways. Mysteriously this plant—one of the most invasive I know—has the common name "obedient plant"!) In the back of the Yellow Bed the yarrow, when in bloom, makes a very effective mass. Moving the yarrow was one of the first jobs I did, in executing my threefold plan, and it is fortunate that I had help, or I would still be at it. Yarrow is beastly stuff to dig—a deep tangle of roots growing every which way, tough as barbed wire. In August, after it stops flowering, I cut the stalks down low to the ground, leaving the attractive ferny gray foliage.

For the back of the Blue Bed, I use all the wild daisies that come up here and there; they are easy to transplant and make a pretty picture when they all flower in late spring, although they're not what you'd call tidy. They

". . . it is a curious thing that people will sometimes spoil some garden project for the sake of a word. For instance, a blue garden, for beauty's sake, may be hungering for a group of white Lilies, or for something of palest lemon-yellow, but it is not allowed to have it because it is called the blue garden, and there must be no flowers in it but blue flowers. I can see no sense in this; it seems to me like fetters foolishly self-imposed. Surely the business of the blue garden is to be beautiful as well as to be blue."

Gertrude Jekyll

135

quit flowering in July, and afterward that side of the border is a Problem. I planted a lot of salvia *(S. praetensis)*, which doesn't really do the job. It's invisible; the dull purplish flower stalks can't be seen from farther than two feet away. One of these days I'll move it somewhere; surely there must be a spot that's crying for invisible flowers?

If truth be told, the Blue Bed is not entirely successful. My husband suggested once that I should stop thinking of it as blue, since it really isn't.

Delphiniums don't grow well for me. (There, I've said it.) I've planted I don't know how many of them, bought from a variety of sources, and they do not last. I can't even blame slugs or woodchucks; nothing eats them, they simply cease to live after their brief flowering. I used to think it was just a case of them being snob flowers that wanted to be in England, or Greenwich, Connecticut, instead of on an old farm in upstate New York, but then my friend Carol, who gardens across the road, planted delphiniums around the silo, and they flourished and have come back year after year; and neighbor Sophie, whose garden is up the hill, grows delphiniums that are taller than I am, and bluer than a July sky. It is a bitter pill for me to swallow.

LIFE IN THE POST-EPIPHANY ERA

I soldier on, battling disappointment along with weeds and drought and Japanese beetles. The Formless Mess still is. This spring I really thought I had it licked. I wrestled with the asters and the physostegia; I divided and conquered the various phloxes, to the extent that there was actual breathing space between the plants. But the day after the first summer thunderstorm I walked out to the border to find that the plants had recaptured all their territory, and then some.

After four summers I still have fewer delphiniums than I want, and more yarrow and orange lilies and monarda and physostegia than I could ever have a use for. The grass creeps into the beds whenever I turn my back. Wild asters emerge, fully grown, on a daily basis. And after all my efforts, the garden still looks most beautiful in early June, when the peonies are blooming.

I've come to accept the fact that—despite the shade problem—the border is after all in the best possible place. For one thing it enjoys the most favorable physical situation, for soil and drainage, on the property; I've noticed that grass surrounding it stays green in the summer when everything else dies. I'd go really crazy (even crazier than I am now) if it were located where I had to look at it all the time; I'd never stop fussing with it. Instead it's more or less in the public eye, which is maybe a good thing. The folks driving by can enjoy the huge drift of yarrow in July, the pinks and reds of the phlox in August; perhaps they get the best of it. At fifty miles an hour it probably looks

". . . if the colors don't seem right . . . move the plants around until you like them better. When you shift things about, you get a good many surprises, and commonly one partner of an especially satisfying color group will promptly die. . . . No matter. We just keep at it, and presumably we will get it all worked out the year after we die."

Henry Mitchell
The Essential
Earthman

137

like a blur of pretty colors. Once a woman stopped and complimented me on the garden, and then—I was on my knees, in my perennial servitude pose, pulling out grass by the roots—she said, "I guess it pretty much takes care of itself, doesn't it?"

No, it doesn't.

I long ago gave up my dream of serenity. Now I dream of more flower gardens. So far the perennial border has spawned at least four offspring. The first was the tulip-clematis-hollyhock border, outside my office window. Then came the nasturtium bed: I love nasturtiums (I'm aware that in some circles yellow flowers are thought vulgar), but I couldn't find a place for them; they don't mix well with the other annuals that I grow on the deck in pots, or in the vegetable garden. So I dug up beds on either side of the entrance to the swimming pool and planted lots of nasturtium seed. I added some of those perennial sunflowers for height and tossed in orange lilies, and extended the border along the fence with black-eyed Susans and coreopsis. But then I planted some mixed achillea I grew from seed, and that was a mistake: they came up in various subtle shades of cream-rose-mauve, not nasturtium-friendly. They'll have to go back into the big border, perhaps to Pink . . .

Then there's the Semi-Wild Garden, in a wooded spot behind the house, which is home to daffodils and Siberian squill and *Tradescantia* and Johnson's blue geranium and violas, and future home to the pulmonaria and columbine, which I've decided are out of place in the original border. However, the white bleeding heart that I planted there turned out to be a mistake—too big, too white—so it's on its way to the Blue Bed.

Just this year I broke ground for yet another bed in a sunny area at the edge of the lawn behind the house. I'll use it as a dump for all the excess yarrow and physostegia and asters (the good asters, like Alma, and those deep violet ones that grow on roadsides), as well as daylilies and perennial sunflowers and goldenrod; all plants whose large size and rough manners make them unfit for consorting with the likes of dianthus and campanula. And near the swimming pool I've set aside a corner that I plan to fill with Russian sage and annual blue salvia and lamb's ears and caryopteris; it will be a blue-silver garden, with no reds or yellows permitted. (At last, Good Taste!)

"Who's in charge here?" I sometimes ask, as I scurry about the property, lugging a wheelbarrow full of bulbs and plants from one garden to another. Sometimes I think of the Perennial Border as a greedy green monster that has enslaved me. At night—even in the winter when it is supposedly sound asleep—I can hear it calling me, whispering suggestions: "If you moved some more of the sunflowers and yarrow out of the Yellow Bed, you could have that blue and yellow garden you always wanted. All it would take would be a few delphiniums . . ."

VEGETABLE BLUES

We love our veggies; they are the freshest, the juiciest, the cutest little veggies on the block. It makes us tingle all over to know that we grew them our very own selves. They have never seen the inside of a truck or supermarket, no label has ever been glued to their dewy cheeks. We even admire their slight imperfections: those little scars and cracks demonstrate our adherence to the organic way.

Nonetheless, raising vegetables, like raising children, isn't *all* bliss. The little darlings have their problems. Sometimes we wonder why we ever got into this mess; sometimes we think longingly of the good old days, buying cellophane-wrapped, California-grown produce at the supermarket.

Occasionally, and strictly among friends, one is known to complain; to tear one's hair and shake one's fist, Job-like. A list of complaints might include—but not be limited to—the following:

WEEDING. Vegetables get more weeds than anything else grown in the garden. There's a reason for this (besides the natural cussedness of the weed): every single thing you do to the land to make it vegetable-friendly encourages weeds.

141

Plowing and tilling the soil to make it loose and crumbly—*friable*—benefits the weeds in so many ways that the little devils probably clap their hands and cheer when they see the Rototiller come out of the barn. Those blades do a great job of root division on the perennial weeds, making many plants out of few. (This only works on weeds; it is not recommended for peonies.) In addition, each time you turn over the earth you're bringing old weed seeds up to the surface, where they can sprout. And that lovely friable dirt is a perfect nursery bed for any weed seed doing a flyover.

Watering and fertilizing also abet the enemy, and so does the very act of *weeding*; every time you pull up one of the little monsters, you're making a window of opportunity for some other plant interloper—after having most likely left a viable section of weed root underground.

HARVESTING. For sheer, brutalizing hard work, nothing beats harvesting. Ask any farm worker. Except that the difference between the field hand and us is that he is at least being paid, however miserably. Also, he probably gets the occasional day off. There's no relief for us gardeners; pick we must, day in and day out, rain or shine.

If you don't pick when the picking is good, dire things may occur: the spinach will go to seed, tomatoes will rot, beans will become tough, corn will fall victim to marauding raccoons, carrots and radishes will turn into wood, broccoli and cauliflower will send up bouquets of bitter yellow flowers, squashes will grow beyond the bounds of propriety . . . The back of your neck turns deepest mahogany brown, while your face—permanently aimed downward—stays pale. This is the Farmer Tan; wear it proudly.

KILLING. All the while you're crawling around the vegetable patch plucking weeds and picking fruit, you are waging a ruthless no-prisoners war on the competition. Swat, squish, splat: another family of Mexican bean beetles, squash vine borers, grasshoppers, cutworms (God's innocent creatures, going about their God-given chores) bites the dust. Oops, was that a spined soldier bug, ally of the gardener, enemy of the Colorado potato beetle? Pity.

Killing, as everyone knows, is progressive; soon we've escalated to woodchucks and rabbits. All our lofty reverence-for-life sentiments turn to dross at the first sighting of a toothmark on a lettuce leaf. To think that we originally got into gardening out of a wish to be closer to the life force: instead of Demeter, maternal goddess of the harvest, our tutelary god has become Kali the destroyer.

WATERING. Vegetable gardens need an inch or more of rain per week in order to thrive. Nowhere in the United States is this condition regularly met, except in those parts of the country that regularly spend their summers submerged by one of our mighty rivers. (This is not appreciated by the crops.)

Hence the garden hose, unquestionably the most hateful device ever invented. Drag the heavy cumbersome thing all the way out to its fullest length (which is six feet short of where you need it), turn it on and nothing happens—there's a kink somewhere. Unkink it and it takes off, spritzing everything in sight, like a water-breathing dragon. Meanwhile its path through the garden is strewn with broken and uprooted plants, victims of its progress.

Besides the common garden hose, there are all kinds of refinements and attachments, and some quite elaborate irrigation systems that the suppliers are willing to sell you. Necessary evils is about the best you can say of any of these devices. Then there's the sprinkler: place it carefully, turn it on and leave it to souse the vegetable patch for a few hours; come back to find it has tipped five degrees to the west and is drenching your open living room window instead.

Every year after the first hard frost, in the midst of all one's sadness at the end of summer and the end of the harvest, there is one moment of unmixed joy: when it comes time to turn off the outdoor hoses, reel them up and put them away. Ahhhh.

TOO MUCH. You know intellectually that a tomato seed the size of a letter on this page has the potential of producing a plant taller than the person reading it, and enough fruit to fill the chair that person is sitting on. You therefore plant six seeds, setting the rest of the package aside for next year (except that you'll forget you have it when the time comes, and order more); and then not one of the seeds comes up. You replant, and this time they all come up, all twelve. You nurse them along, through various childhood crises, telling yourself that any day you'll thin out the less vigorous plants, but they're all so feeble-looking it's hard to make a cull. Finally you put them out in the ground, and half of them die, so that's all right. Tomato hornworms and other unspeakable critters attack, stripping the poor puny seedlings of all their leaves. Weird diseases wreak havoc, while alternating droughts and thunderstorms further decimate the crop. In July, as the neighbors begin to boast of ripening fruit, you realize you haven't yet seen any blossoms. It's beginning to look like a non-tomato summer. Despairing, you turn your back on the garden for a few days.

That thundering you hear is the sound of hundreds of ripe tomatoes falling off the vines and rolling across the lawn to batter down your kitchen door.

Now, there is nothing more wonderful to eat than a just-picked ripe tomato, still warm from the vine. Slice it thick, sprinkle it with a little salt and eat it in a sandwich, standing over the sink with the juice running down your face. Mmmmm. Or cut it up and let it marinate for an hour in olive oil, salt and plenty of chopped-up garlic and basil; then spread it on lightly browned Italian bread, and call it *bruschetta.* Or take the same mix and toss it with cooked spaghetti, and top it with some fine Parmesan. Or layer sliced tomatoes with fresh mozzarella and basil leaves, and drizzle olive oil and balsamic vinegar over all. Or chunk them up in the blender with your other summer produce—cucumbers, onions, peppers sweet and hot, herbs—for a refreshing gazpacho. And then there are all the different ways of using cooked tomatoes; there must be an infinite number of uses for this versatile fruit.

Unfortunately, one's *capacity* for tomatoes is finite. With the

145

RECIPE FOR TOMATO SAUCE

I've tried for years to find an easy way to preserve the huge glut of tomatoes that we harvest every year. The problem is that when they are cooked, tomatoes deconstruct into three not very desirable elements: seeds, skin and water. I have a hand-cranked gismo from Italy (mine is called Suprema Pomodoro) that separates the seeds and skin from the watery pulp, which must then be cooked down; this is a fairly labor-intensive operation, though vastly easier than using an ordinary food mill. A few years ago I hit upon the idea of grilling the tomatoes first; this reduces the water content while giving them a rich, smoky taste. It also means that I can do most of the work outside. This is a two-person job.

Millions of ripe tomatoes, halved; stems and blemishes removed

Salt	*Bay leaves*	*Pepper*
Olive oil	*Garlic*	*Basil (optional)*

Fire up the grill. When it is ready, start grilling the tomatoes, turning them from time to time. They are done when the skins blacken and they begin to bubble. As they cook, transfer them to a tomato grinder or a food mill to extract the skin and seeds. Continue until all the tomatoes are finished. Put the resulting pulp into a big pot with a little salt; about ¼ cup olive oil to each quart of pulp; a couple of bay leaves; and plenty of crushed peeled garlic cloves. Cook slowly, stirring as needed, until reduced by half. (This will take an hour or more and is a good time not to be in the kitchen.) When reduced, taste; remove bay leaves, add pepper and salt if needed.

At this point you could either freeze the sauce, or:

Pour sauce into sterilized canning jars (8 ounces is a good size), adding a sprig of basil to each, then process in boiling water according to manufacturer's directions.

best will in the world, it is not humanly possible to consume more than, perhaps, five tomatoes in a day. And after a five-tomato day, you may need a few zero-tomato days. Meanwhile the pile of tomatoes on the kitchen table gets higher, and riper, every day. (No, you can't put them in the refrigerator.)

The same problem occurs with most of the other vegetables we grow. The absolute cucumber limit is even less: maybe one-half cuke per person, per day. Zucchinis are, of course, notorious for overproduction. If you don't run out and pick them almost hourly, they burgeon into great inedible club-like things that no one wants to eat—but because you grew them you're obliged to use them, and as long as the kitchen table is groaning under the weight of all that home-grown produce you can't go out and purchase any. Why, to *buy* carrots, say, from a farm stand, while you've got carrots (however puny and misshapen) growing in your own garden, would be equivalent to adultery!

So what's to be done with the excess? God knows you can't give it away—everyone else has too many eggplants at exactly the same time as you; this is the nature of vegetable gardening.

You could get a pig. Or you could try to sell your excess bounty. One year while

RECIPE FOR PICKLED BEANS

I'm fanatic about snap beans; I pick them every day—sometimes twice a day—so as to get them small and skinny, which is the only way they are worth eating. (I grow both French filet beans and some American varieties, which when picked young are just as good. The Americans bear more heavily in my garden, but—this is strange but true—the Japanese beetles leave the French beans alone. If left on the vine to the point where they become thick and tough, I'll leave them to ripen until the seeds inside mature, when they can be eaten as shell beans—which also make wonderful eating.) In late July, when the beans first start coming in, there are so many of them, it's nice to have a way of preserving them that is easy and tasty; this truly is something we enjoy eating even in the winter. The beans retain their crispness and make a nice low-cal cocktail snack.

For each 12-ounce jar:
½ pound fresh young snap beans, washed and stemmed
*   (if they're at all limp, refresh them in ice water for an hour)*
1 peeled clove garlic
½ teaspoon dill seed
½ small hot pepper, such as jalapeño
1 cup white vinegar
1 cup water
1 tablespoon salt

Pack the beans lengthwise into the sterilized jars, crowding them in tightly, allowing ½ inch of space at the top. Add garlic, dill and hot pepper.

Bring vinegar, water and salt to a full boil, and pour into jars, up to ¼ inch from rim. Secure lids and process in boiling water for 10 minutes according to manufacturer's directions. Remove the garlic and pepper before serving. Serve chilled.

we were still gardening in Fire Island we had a bumper crop of cucumbers. We grew them in big planter boxes on the deck, training the vines up the wall of the house, where they peeked in the bathroom window, startling our guests. There was so much fruit that year that I used to take a few with me whenever I went out, in case I met someone who needed a cucumber. Finally I brought some to my local grocer and asked if he wanted to try selling them. He could and did, and for a few days I had the pleasure of seeing them in the vegetable display; I even earned a couple of dollars. Then the cucumbers quit production all of a sudden—my husband was convinced that they were insulted at being used commercially—and that was the end of my career as a market gardener. I've never again had much success growing cukes.

PRESERVING. If in midsummer country roads are clogged with gardeners driving carloads of vegetable largesse from house to house, looking in vain for a recipient, late summer finds them bumper to bumper with gardeners trying to give away sticky little jars of tomato chutney and pickled zucchini.

I hate canning. (Which doesn't mean that I don't do it, every year.) Canning requires that you fill your kitchen with steam for long hours, at the hottest time of the year, on a day when all sensible humans are at the beach or lying in a hammock.

Canning and preserving, allegedly economical practices, require a hefty initial outlay for all those jars and lids and pots and racks, not to mention the special sugars and spices and vinegars. If you haven't yet started preserving, you might weigh the cost of the paraphernalia against the value of a few jars of eggplant ketchup.

It's also a potentially deadly hobby, with the frightening spectre of botulism hovering over the operation. This is not a field for culinary experimentation. If you don't follow the directions exactly, you and your loved ones may turn up on the six o'clock news: "A local family collapsed today after a picnic, felled by homemade zucchini marmalade . . ."

Freezing your vegetable bounty doesn't carry the same risk as canning, but somehow a freezer full of plastic containers isn't as impressive or as decorative as a row of colorful mason jars filled with your very own relishes and preserves. Those jars are handy as hostess gifts (cheaper than a bottle of wine!); bringing someone a Ziploc bag of frozen string beans isn't quite the same.

TIMING. It's a nice warm June day, you go out to the lettuce patch to pick some greens for lunch and—what's this? The lettuce, perfect two days ago, has sent up a stalk a foot high, and before you try to taste it your nose tells you it's turned bitter. Yank it up and toss it on the compost heap, it's history. The lettuce has "bolted." This is the plant's attempt to make a flower head and set seed, selfishly thinking of its progeny and the future of its gene pool, instead of your lunch. Never mind that you like to eat salad in the summer; the salad has its own timetable.

Bad timing plagues the home vegetable gardener. Radishes, summer food if anything is, hate growing in hot weather. Two nights of over eighty-degree temperatures, and they're outta there. Meanwhile the garden is merrily turning out turnips and beets that nobody will want to look at until November. Even tomatoes, which we crave in the early summer months, don't really hit their stride until the end of August. Swiss chard: ripe in August, in demand in October. Red onions: harvest in September, not needed until May. Cauliflower and broccoli: ready in August, not on the menu until cold weather sets in. Pumpkins: ready by Labor Day, rotting by Halloween.

Last summer I made tons of salsa, using my own hot peppers and tomatoes and cilantro (though I did have to go to the store for the limes and the vinegar and the salt and the jars and the lids). The salsa was fine, but it's still sitting on the shelf. The problem is, I don't want to eat salsa in the winter. I won't want to eat it until July, when I'll be able to make fresh salsa, but I'll have to eat the old stuff because I made it—and grew it—so I can't throw the jars out. (Maybe I'll tie red ribbons on them and give them away at Christmas.)

NOT ENOUGH. It goes without saying that a feast will be followed by a famine. One week ago you had a bumper crop of arugula; the refrigerator was crammed with the stuff, you gave sacks of it to your friends, you made soup with it, you considered opening a roadside stand. Now you're having a dinner party, and you don't have so much as one leaf to serve to the guests. You have to go to the store and buy it, and then explain lamely to your friends that if only they'd come last week . . . (And meanwhile there's lots of kale.)

You could have avoided this by planting arugula seeds every week, but you didn't. Or the rain washed the seeds away, or the flea beetles ravaged the leaves, or the weather turned hot and it bolted.

The sad and bitter truth is, having a vegetable garden—even a big one—doesn't guarantee that you'll have fresh produce on the table when you want it. Just because you gave those vegetables life, nurtured them from seed to fruit, spent the better part of the summer on your knees pulling weeds and eliminating predators, doesn't mean they'll dance to your tune. They have their own agenda.

Vegetable gardening does have satisfactions, not the least of which is the fun of sharing gripes with other neophyte farmers. The depradations of the raccoons; the glut of cucumbers and the dearth of peppers; the drought, the flood, the hailstorm that smashed the pole beans; the tenacity of the dandelions; the mysterious discolorations on the tomato cheeks; the failure to set fruit of the eggplant. Whatever would we find to talk about at cocktail parties without these absorbing subjects? And if, in between laments, we allow ourselves an occasional boast—a quiet mention that never has one tasted cauliflower so luscious, so flavorful, as this year's, could it be the compost?—God knows we have earned these small triumphs.

THE GOOD EARTH, AND THE NOT SO GOOD

There comes a time in the life of every gardener when she or he must take a good hard look at that brown stuff underfoot. Most of the time one ignores it; after all, gardening by its nature consists of covering all that with things that are more beautiful or more useful. If a bare patch suddenly appears in the middle of the yard, one plunks a plant or some seeds into it, waters it and hopes not to see that naked earth ever again.

Then disaster strikes. An expensive shrub dies or fails to flower, and the nursery that was happy to sell it to us last year now informs us we should never have been trusted with it in the first place.

"But I watered it exactly the way you said, I planted it in a beautiful spot, not too deep and not too shallow; I protected it from the winter wind and the summer drought, I even talked to it," you whine. And they ask:

"What kind of soil do you have?"

What do you mean, "What kind of soil"? It's brown, it supports my weight, things grow in it. Isn't this enough?

No, it isn't enough. The right stuff is rich black loam, teeming

"The perfect garden soil is a balanced mixture of five constituents: of solids perhaps two-thirds rock particles, of sizes ranging from small stones down to the tiniest specks of clay; one-third animal and vegetable matter, mainly dead and decayed but with a substantial population of living creatures; a considerable quantity of water and a remarkable amount of air. Unfortunately it is a rare occurrence for such a soil to form naturally."

Hugh Johnson
The Principles of
Gardening

with worms. It is friable; it has tilth; it drains like a dream. It consists of just the right mix of sand and clay and silt, and contains ample amounts of the Big Three nutrients (nitrogen, phosphorus and potassium), as well as all the known and unknown lesser ones. Its pH is impeccable. Its texture is so light and fluffy you could use it as a pillow. Its structure permits plant roots to grow deep and strong, and to help themselves to all the water and oxygen they need. Good soil is chock-full of humus, which is the end product of decaying vegetable and animal matter. (This is a good thing. Really.) This is soil to fall upon and kiss, the Platonic Ideal of soil.

And then there are all the others: just as happy families are alike and unhappy families differ, soils can be bad in a depressing variety of ways.

What I have, on my property, is clay mixed with gravel on top of hardpan. Think "parking lot" and you'll get the picture. It doesn't fry, and when you try to till it the tiller bends, although it does drain pretty well. I would call it dirt rather than soil.

Still, it's not *all* bad, as mothers say of their jailbird sons. Worms like it. It is good at growing some things: tulips, raspberries, tomatoes, beans, sunflowers, phlox, peonies, etc., all bear prodigiously. It even grows rhododendrons, although it utterly refused to provide a home for the lovely little magnolia I planted the first year.

I muddled along with my dirt for several years, taking the good with the bad, but then the time came when I had to get scientific. It was the vegetable garden—our *fourth* vegetable garden on this property—that drove me to it.

A Digression

Before getting down to the nitty-gritty, I should explain the why and how of the four vegetable gardens.

The first was a big sloppy vegetable plot behind the house, smack in the middle of the view; it was there when we bought the house. We plowed it under at the end of the first year and dug a new garden. Garden Two was across the road—no danger of it offending visually—and smaller: maybe two hundred square feet. We thought we didn't need or want a big vegetable garden. We were wrong.

A couple of years later when it became evident that the new garden was much too small—and too far away, *and* across the road—we built Garden Three on a slope off to the right of the house. Now we had plenty of growing space—about nine hundred square feet—but the steepness of the site made for problems. Hobbling up and down the rows as I weeded and cultivated, I felt like an Andean peasant farmer—except that my body hadn't had generations of Andean peasant ancestors to enable it to function in that bent-over posture. The other problem was, of course, our old friend the soil: it was pale, hard and gravelly, like a steep parking lot. Some of my vegetables were less than wonderful; some of them simply weren't. I added manure and topsoil, but because of the slope the good stuff washed away with every rain. Rather than construct a lot of elaborate earthworks to correct the grade, we moved it again. (One friend speculated that it must have been quite a job to keep digging up and replanting all those carrots and beets and onions.)

Keeping Garden Three as a pumpkin-and-sunflower patch, we located Garden Four on what seemed an ideal site. It was near the house (but not in the view) on almost level land with good southern exposure, far from competing tree roots, in a field that had been used for generations as cow pasture, presumably giving it a head start in the manure department. This ultimate garden was to be the biggest yet: fourteen hundred square feet. I put a great deal of thought and study into its design, filling page after page of graph paper with plans. I envisioned a sort of post-modern *potager,* with flowers and vegetables in luxuriant rows, beauty and function ineluctably fused.

Work on Garden Four began in the autumn. A *lot* of work. Together with a friend, my husband constructed a formidable anti-woodchuck fence with two gates to surround the plot. We plowed (or, I should say, paid a man with a tractor to plow), and then we laid out paths and built raised vegetable beds, leaving room in the center of the garden for a birdbath in a circle of herbs.

After Garden Four was finished, almost as an afterthought, I decided to see if the soil was any good.

156

CHEMISTRY

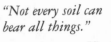

Using a kit (Sudbury Soil Test: $15.99 at the hardware store), I tested the soil and compared the results with the old site up on the hill. To my surprise, the soils of Gardens Three and Four were almost identical: both had middling pH and moderate but not spectacular levels of nutrients. Disappointed but not yet worried, I bought several truckloads of manure, both the cow and the horse variety, which we dug into the raised beds—*hard work*—before covering them with a blanket of leaves for the winter.

"Not every soil can bear all things."

Virgil

Come spring I rushed outside, armed with hoe and rake and seed packages, to find—hard pale clay, mixed with gravel, on top of hardpan; more like a parking lot than a garden. Seedlings planted that spring withered, small seeds never broke through the crust. Throughout the season, the success/failure rate was about half and half, and some of the plants that usually do very well were terrible disappointments. The onions were half-size.

I pulled out the test kit again at the end of the season. The pH seemed a bit higher (7.0); everything else was the same.

157

I needed an expert opinion. I gathered samplings of dirt from various locations around the vegetable plot—from the bed where the leeks were performing brilliantly, from the one where the cabbages had fallen victim to bugs, and from the one where repeated sowings of zinnia seed had failed to see the light of day—and put them all together in a bag and took them and $15 to my county extension office for an official analysis. Two weeks later a computer printout—my garden dirt's report card—arrived in the mail.

I'm not sure what I'd been hoping for. An oracle? A set of simple instructions? What I got was a lot of numbers. The pH was 7.1. (Normal range is 6.0–7.5.) The other readings were even less meaningful. Is it good or bad to get a 39 in manganese, a 2.3 in zinc? Is 3.9% organic matter enough? Should I be worried that I have 6 pounds of iron an acre—or proud? It was like having a horoscope done and being told that you have three planets in your sixth house, when you want to know whether or not you should get married. The only concrete advice was the suggestion that I "apply 2 lbs of 10-6-4 per 100 sq ft," and that I refrain from adding lime or anything that would further elevate the pH.

I do think it is mean, at this stage of my life, to have to confront chemistry again: a subject I thought I had put behind after an ignominious encounter in high school. This pH business, for instance: I just can't grasp it. I know pH measures the acidity-alkalinity of your soil; I know that in the real world 7.0 is neutral, but in the world of gardens 6.0 is the ideal. All the books I've read insist that having the right pH is crucial—and then they go on to acknowledge that most plants can tolerate a wide range of pH values. This "worry/don't worry" business could drive a person nuts.

After puzzling over my report card for a few weeks, I finally called the county cooperative-extension office and asked for illumination. The actual agent was away (on a case?), but a nice man in the office explained things to me; it was like discussing blood-test results with your doctor's nurse. He quickly set my mind at rest about the zinc and the manganese, and although he seemed as mystified as I was about the line in the printout that read "Salts 9mnho/cm): 0.200," he assured me it wasn't anything to be concerned about. He told me my soil has a fair amount of nutrients, but that 3.9% organic matter is not so hot: 10% to 15% is more like it. The elevated pH was "something to watch." (Like a middling-high cholesterol count.) The bottom line was this: I had to add more stuff to the soil, preferably rotting stuff. Having taken food out of the garden—even though the food wasn't exactly state-fair caliber—it was now my duty to put something back. But what?

I could add mountains of peat moss, which would help to lighten the clay and to lower the pH, but I'm not crazy about peat moss. It is the driest, thirstiest substance on the planet and must be thoroughly mixed with water before it can be used—more hard work—else it

"It takes a huge effort to change soil texture. For example, to have a beneficial effect on clayey soil in a 20 x 50 garden bed, you'd have to add about 3-5 tons of sand to the top 6" of soil."

Rodale's All-New
Encyclopedia of
Organic Gardening

*Behold this compost!
behold it well!
Perhaps every mite
has once form'd
part of a sick per-
son—yet behold!
The grass of spring
covers the prairies,
The bean bursts
noiselessly through
the mould in the
garden,
The delicate spear of
the onion pierces
upward,
The apple-buds clus-
ter together on the
apple-branches,
The resurrection of
the wheat appears
with pale visage
out of its graves,*

*The summer growth
is innocent and
disdainful above
all those strata of
sour dead.*

What chemistry!...

Walt Whitman,
"This Compost," from
Leaves of Grass

will steal moisture from the plants. In envi-
ronmental circles, using peat moss is now
frowned upon, as it is a nonrenewable resource
like petroleum. It costs money, too.

Sand is sometimes used to improve soil,
but there's a danger that if you don't use
enough, or if you use too much, it can make
it worse; even *more* like a parking lot. Too
risky.

The answer to all my problems was, in a
word, compost, that miracle stuff that everyone—but me—has a bin of in their backyard.
Compost is the new cure-all, the sweetheart of
the organically minded. Add it to your garden
and it will take care of whatever ails it: lighten
heavy soils, enrich barren ones, improve drainage, correct pH, nourish earthworms, and all
but guarantee bumper crops.

CONFESSION

I'm a failure at compost.

This is not an easy admission. Making
compost is probably the single greenest thing
you can do. When I tell people that I have a
country place, the first thing they ask, even
before "Do you have a garden?" and "How
many animals do you have?" is: "Do you have
a compost heap?" Composting leaves and

lawn clippings and table scraps is the ultimate good: it turns a sin—wastefulness—into a virtue. I'd dearly love to belong to this club, but I can't.

I've been trying, in one location or another, to make compost most of my life. Once I was almost successful: my husband and I had a country place in western New Jersey—it was near the town of Hope and we called the place "Beyond Hope," which gives you some idea—and I piled up grass clippings and leaves and kitchen waste, the way you're supposed to, and lo and behold, it did what *it* was supposed to do; it heated up and began to smoke. And then Don built a brush fire next to it—I know not why—and the smoke became a full-fledged fire, and that was the end of that batch of compost.

Mostly what happens is I put all the ingredients in a heap or a bin, and water it and turn it as much as I can, and months and years go by and the pile just sits there: a collection of perfectly recognizable weeds and leaves and peelings and rinds and egg shells and apple cores and rotten onions and withered flowers; in short, garbage. It never progresses past the slimy, smelly stage. And if I add manure to encourage it (although this seems wrong

"If Gardener's Supply could leave but one legacy, we'd want it to be that we've significantly increased the amount of compost being made in America. In the past 60 years, 50% of our topsoil has been washed away, killed with chemicals, or paved over. Making good compost is the only reliable shortcut to rebuilding humus and soil fertility . . ."

Advertisement for Gardener's Supply Company

somehow, wouldn't it make more sense to put the manure directly into the garden?), or lime, or dirt, or whatever the pundits say to add, the additives just sit there, too. And much as I try to keep twigs and stalks out of the heap, when I try to stick a shovel into one of my old compost heaps (there are several of them, around the world), it can't penetrate very far because of all the woody stems. It is possible that the only alchemy taking place here is that of soft leaves and stems becoming stiff and tough. I even purchased a product, sort of a compost helper (Ringer makes it and it is called *Recycle Compost Plus, extra strength for hard to compost materials*), and I scattered some of it in my latest attempt at compost, which is in a hole in the vegetable garden, but I have little faith in it.

Lack of faith could be my problem, but I don't think it is. My problem is laziness. Every article or book ever written about making compost contains the sentence (often in the title): "Making compost is easy!" And then they go on to explain at great length all the steps you have to take to make this magical substance, without which you cannot ever hold your head up among friends of the environment. Some of these "Perfect Compost in 30

Easy Days" books are hundreds of pages long!

Then there are all the special products: the bins and the tumblers to enclose your compost; the gadgets you hook up to your mower so it collects the all-important grass clippings, and the shredders to chop up leaves and branches. "Easy cheap compost" could cost an arm and a leg! There are also devices that you stick into the heap to aerate it, which is one of the vital steps in transforming garbage into "brown gold." (As anyone can tell you who has tried it, turning a huge heap of not-yet-compost with a pitchfork is worse than back-breaking; it is impossible.) If your heap isn't on the ground, you'll need to add some red worms. You'll also want to buy a special "hot-bed soil thermometer" so you'll know when the heap is cooked enough.

Compost begins to sound like an end in itself. In an editorial in *National Gardening,* Jack Ruttle admits—*boasts*—that making compost is "the part of the garden that takes more of my time than the roses, the apples, the perennial beds or any of the vegetables." Mowing and weeding and leaf-raking have become a matter of harvesting raw materials for the all-important heap: ". . . forget about the turning. Just *building* a pile that big ('three feet

"In the bad old days before recycling, a composting fanatic could easily get a couple of pickup loads of neatly bagged leaves each fall. The neighbors were doing all the work. Same thing in spring with grass clippings. It was a composter's paradise! Today I have to collect my own clippings—I mow more for the compost and mulch than for the lawn. And I have to scythe huge amounts of weeds to layer with the clippings."

Jack Rattle,
in National Gardening,
March/April 1994

163

"I don't like to make fun of anybody, even including my betters, but I do have to smile sometimes at the mental convolutions the experts are going through in regard to compost piles. Do this, don't do that, put on this, not too little, but be careful, not too much; wet it, but not too wet; now— no, we've changed our minds, this is better. Now we've got it—no, wait a minute—"

Ruth Stout
How to Have a Green
Thumb Without an
Aching Back

wide, three feet high and six feet long'—of end product) takes a lot of stuff."

If you actually read those "Joy of Compost" books, you learn that it is by no means a simple process. To begin with, there are two kinds of compost. The kind I've been failing to create is Cold. Pile it up, stir it occasionally, and some-day it will metamorphose into that elusive brown gold; the theory being that eventually everything—including thee and me—rots. Everything except my compost.

For Hot compost (this is the kind that heats up enough to kill weed seeds) you have to stack the stuff in layers; so many inches of brown (carbon), so many of green (nitrogen), with an occasional shovelful of dirt—rather like making a very large, very heavy lasagna.

All the mavens agree that the ultimate pile must be big; how big is a matter of de-bate. Brown is leaves and stems and straw; green is grass and weeds and table scraps. Cof-fee grounds aren't brown, they are green. News-paper is brown, manure is green. Got it? The ratio between the two must be just right—but no two experts quite agree on what is right. To do it properly you should start with a big mound of brown and another of green, and then build it all at one time. Then, after a few weeks or months of faithful watering and stirring, it will be "done." Good luck.

Manure

Animal manure is supposed to have all the wonderful properties of compost, and then some. Well-aged cow manure is the ideal, and if it is also dried, so much the better. You can buy this splendid stuff in plastic bags at any garden center, for a price.

For a lesser price, you can get it from your neighboring farm, if you have one. Pigs, sheep, chickens, horses and bats also manufacture manure. In fact, all God's children do; but there are good reasons, besides squeamishness, not to use human or pet droppings in the garden: they may carry disease or parasites. A pile of fresh aromatic steaming excrement, whatever the animal, is *not* the best thing for your plants. The high ammonia content can burn them. Also, raw manure may be full of weed seeds. On the other hand, very old manure may have lost its zip. Buying manure is a lot like buying wine. If it is too young, you can stash it in a corner of the garden—upwind— and wait a year or so before uncorking it.

". . . the scene is an elevator in the Brill Building . . .

Thin Guy: This afternoon, I've got to look for a Valentine gift for my wife.

Heavyset, Bearded Guy: My wife only wants a wheelbarrow and some manure for Valentine's Day. She also wants a roto-tiller, but that has to wait.

Thin Guy: You live on a farm?

Heavyset, Bearded Guy: God no! Upper West Side."

"Metropolitan Diary," in The New York Times, February 10, 1993

"*Veterinarian Richard Stelmach has a bountiful supply of dog droppings. . . . Dick digs a foot-deep hole to bury the droppings, covers them with soil, and then plants the tomatoes on top. 'It made a big difference,' he notes. 'Also, it's probably better for the environment if it doesn't go to the dump.'* "

Shelley Goldbloom
Garden Smarts

Another way to boost the organic content of your soil is to plant something called Green Manure: a cover crop which, when it is subsequently plowed into the soil, will add nutrients. As I write this, a bag of winter rye seed sits on my kitchen windowsill, waiting to be planted in the vegetable garden, as recommended by the nice man at the cooperative extension office. The idea is to sow it in the fall; the plants come up and act as sort of a living mulch over the winter, protecting the ground from erosion and compaction, and then in the spring you dig them into the earth to add that certain organic je ne sais quoi.

The reason the rye seed is on the windowsill and not in the ground is part laziness, part fear. Before I can plant this magic stuff, I'll have to pull up all the weeds and spent plants in the garden. I'll also have to do a fair amount of tilling and raking and watering, all efforts that I associate more with spring than fall. And then—this is the fear—what if, in April, the green manure doesn't *want* to be pulled up? What if I'm away that week, or it's raining or snowing, and by the time I get to the garden it's overgrown with winter rye?

Notions and Potions

If fear and laziness prevail, that bag of winter rye seed will wind up on a shelf in the potting shed, there to keep company with all the other products I've bought over the years because they promised to turn my dirt into soil. (I suppose I can throw out those bags of lime now.)

There are all kinds of fertilizers here, but not one of them is the 10-6-4 formula prescribed by the extension office. (What the numbers mean: the first is Nitrogen, or N, which helps plants make green leaves and lush growth; the second, P, is Phosphorus, good for flowers and fruit and roots; the third, K, is Potassium (sometimes called Potash), which gives plants the strength they need to fight disease and stress. The numbers tell you what percentage of each nutrient is present in the product: a bag of 20-20-20 contains twice as much of everything as a bag of 10-10-10. This is how to remember them: Nitrogen, Phosphorus, Potassium are in alphabetical order. Phosphorus, being first, gets to be called P. Potassium is K because it just is.)

Some of the fertilizers in my collection are: Plant-Tone (5-3-3), Peters (20-20-20), Triple Super Phosphate (0-46-0), Bulb-Tone

"'My grandma lives on a two-hundred-acre farm with lots of pines, which attract deer,' says Linda George Olson . . .'Grandma gathers the deer pellets and mixes them with water for fertilizer.'"

Shelley Goldbloom
Garden Smarts

The stable yields a stercoraceous heap, Impregnated with quick fermenting salts.

William Cowper, "The Garden," 1785

(4-10-6), Holly-Tone (4-6-4), Sea Mix (3-2-2), Rose-Tone (6-6-4), Miracid (30-10-10), Alaskan Fish Fertilizer (5-1-1), Bone Meal (4-12-0), Blood Meal (12-0-0) and Osmocote (18-6-12). Most of these substances are organic because I'm trying to be good, or at least green. The Peters and the Miracid, which are soluble synthetics, are for those emergencies—such as yellow leaves—when a fast fix is needed. The Osmocote is a slow-release fertilizer: you sprinkle the little capsules on the ground and they slowly add their magic to the garden; it's like taking an all-night cold pill.

A question: If I used four pounds of 5-3-3 Plant-Tone per 100 square feet, wouldn't that be almost as good as two pounds of 10-6-4? Maybe I could replicate the exact formula by combining so much Fish Fertilizer, so much Blood Meal, and a soupçon of Bone Meal. It would be popular with the local carnivores; when I use the fish juice, my cats follow me around the garden licking up spills, and some nocturnal beast, attracted by the smell, dug up daffodil bulbs when I planted them with bone meal. What might blood meal bring? Hyenas? Buzzards?

All the books warn of the dangers of overdoing fertilizers, especially the nonorganics:

dangerous buildups of "salts" can result. (There are those mysterious salts again.) Worse still, overdosing on those elusive micronutrients may send your pH spinning out of control. I guess the safest course would be to go to my neighboring Agway and buy some 10-6-4 if they have it; but then I'll never clear out the shed.

Those same shelves are groaning under the weight of an anthology of elixirs and nostrums with names like Super-Sea-Secret. These aren't fertilizers; they are "bio-catalysts" and "enzyme potentiators"; they're chock-full of algae and kelp and "humic extract." I use these potions semireligiously, which is to say in the same spirit as throwing spilled salt over my left shoulder. Most of them must be measured and mixed with water, which is why the potting shed contains both measuring cups and measuring spoons, and even an eyedropper. During planting season I go around mumbling "Two ounces equals four tablespoons"; or is it "Two tablespoons equals one half ounce"? It's like cooking but without the sensory gratification. Arithmetic is a subject, like chemistry, that I thought I'd left behind me long ago. Sometimes I want to just dump all the bags and bottles and cans into the ground and let the ingredients fight it out. (How to turn a cow pasture into a toxic dump in two easy years.)

BEYOND PH

Hoping to learn more about soil-dirt-earth, I attended a lecture at the New York Horticultural Society. The speaker, William Bryant Logan, had studied with Dr. Hans Jenny, "the dean of American soil scientists." This was an entirely different world, far from the realm of pH and N-P-K and manure.

"Just as the sky links outer space to the earth's surface with increasingly dense layers of atmosphere, so does soil link the surface of the earth to planetary bedrock with increasingly dense layers called, appropriately, horizons. Where the bottom layer of the sky rubs up against the top horizon of the soil, almost all terrestrial life is found."

William Bryant Logan, in The New York Times, *June 20, 1993*

Logan told us that Dr. Jenny used to say that trying to understand soil by doing a chemical analysis was akin to trying to understand a human being by cutting off a finger, grinding it up and putting it in a test tube. Evidently the doctor was much given to zen-like pronouncements. Upon watching a dog kicking dirt into a pile, he said, "That is not yet a soil," meaning (I think) that the elements were in disorder—scrambled like the soil sample I took to the extension office.

I learned that there are 14,000 individually named soils; they have science fiction-character names like Myakka and Resota, and are grouped in such categories as *haplahumod* and *haplaquod*. Far from being inert, soil swarms with myriad microscopic creatures that labor tirelessly, transforming death and corruption into life. It is built in strata, or horizons, which come in contrasting colors like the geologic layers in the Grand Canyon.

I saw that the ground under our feet is as complex and unknowable as outer space. As I left the lecture hall, I felt that I had learned a lot—and that I now knew even less about the subject than I had beforehand.

For a while after that I was almost too much in awe of the earth to consider rudely sticking a spade into it. But I recovered; ineffable, numinous though it might be, my garden dirt has a job to do.

THE NITTY-GRITTY

I was finally able to reach my actual cooperative extension agent, Mr. Joel Allen, by phone. (He's a busy guy.) He said that the various grades on my report card were mostly within normal range: the equivalent of a 3.0 index; respectable, but not enough to get you into graduate school.

But I do have two problems: the pH is too high, the organic content is too low. Peat moss might help to lower the pH to a more desirable 6.5; if not that, sulfur. I told him what I had learned from a local farmer: this area used to have such alkaline soil that they had to apply sulfur every year, but that in recent years acid rain had taken care of it. Mr. Allen wasn't buying: "Acid rain affects the water and the trees but not the soil," he told me.

As for fertilizer, he didn't think I had to be religious about the 10-6-4; the main thing was to bump up the available nitrogen, with animal manure in the spring, green manure in the fall. He recommended a cover crop of perennial rye, which sounded alarming, I thought. "It's not *really* perennial," he said—further confusing me—but it is crucial to till it into the soil in early spring, before it starts growing again. When I told him about the two pounds of winter rye on the windowsill, bought for a dollar from a bin at the local hardware store, *he* became alarmed: "Find out what percentage of weed seed it contains!"

What about all the manure already in the soil, I wondered: all the expensive cow end-product we'd purchased, the six pickup-

"When selecting land, do not be deceived by any one who tells you that if not naturally good, the soil may be made so by cultivation and manure. These will help, certainly, but only as education improves the shallow mind. Luxuriant crops can no more be expected from a thin and poor soil— no matter how much it is cultivated— than fertile ideas from a shallow brain, educate it as you will."

Peter Henderson
Gardening for Profit,
1874

truckloads of ordure we'd shoveled and hauled from a horse farm in Massachusetts? What about the one hundred and sixty years of cow dung that had soaked into the field before we started gardening there? Shouldn't it have had *some* impact on the organic content of the soil?"

"More," was the agent's response. "You need to add more."

I love to read accounts of gardeners who turn barren wastelands—actual parking lots in some cases—into fecund paradises. *Organic Gardening* often runs these stories, with Before and After photos, and I find them riveting. They are the gardening equivalent to the "makeover" articles in *Cosmopolitan,* in which sullen, photogenically challenged young women are given a new hairdo and a professional makeup job, and are then photographed, smiling, looking gorgeous, by Francesco Scavullo.

This is why I buy those elixirs of seaweed; this is why I shovel dung, and try once again to make compost. This is why I probably will plant that rye (and then worry about it all winter), and then buy a king's ransom's worth of peat moss. But sometimes I wonder.

Can it be that good soil is like good looks, something you really have to be born with?

CONSIDER THE ONION

I grow a lot of different vegetables; I have a weakness for exotic, offbeat, even funny-looking varieties.

Although my taste in flowers is fairly conservative—I mistrust novelties and prefer old-fashioned blooms that are the color God intended for them—when it comes to vegetables I go for weird. Purple beans, yellow tomatoes, blue squash, red lettuce are all at home here; and if, besides being purple-and-white-striped, the eggplant is shaped like a boomerang, so much the better. (Funnily enough, these often turn out to be the heirlooms.) I also cultivate the foreign-born: my garden is more likely to contain pumpkins from France, tomatoes from Italy and peppers from Mexico, than the familiar, shall we say *garden* varieties. I'm not just being a food snob; I think it makes sense to grow things that are either expensive to buy or difficult to find.

However, if I had to name a favorite garden vegetable, I'd choose the common onion.

The first time I planted them, I was underwhelmed. With onions one begins with either a set—which is a wee immature onion—or a transplant, a skinny scallion-like plant. Either way, it's a case of plant an onion, get an onion. Compared with the miracle of seed—

Let first the onion
 flourish there,
Rose among roots,
 the maiden-fair,
Wine-scented and
 poetic soul
Of the capacious
 salad bowl.

Robert Louis Stevenson,
 "To a Gardener,"
 1887

one tiny dot of matter transmogrifying into a plant bearing dozens of fruits, each one containing hundreds of seeds—this seemed like a pretty dull business. As I stood up from planting them that first spring, I said, Never again.

But then they won my heart by performing so well. The attractive succulent greens soon came up, every one, forming a nice straight row. Elsewhere entire beds of lettuce simply didn't germinate, a hundred radish seeds—planted in a neat line, perfectly spaced—all popped up in one six-inch tangle.

Over the summer fierce dramas took place in the rest of the garden—the cabbages decimated overnight by a woodchuck, tomatoes stunted because of God-knows-which blight, zucchini doomed by the dread squash vine borer—but the onions grew uneventfully, troubled only by a few weeds. At the end of August the tops yellowed, signaling that the bulbs were ready to harvest. No sweat: in a tenth of the time it would take to harvest one bean bush, I pulled all the onions up and left them to dry in the field for a few days before bringing them into the house. Fresh, they were astonishing, at the same time sweet, juicy and pungent; nothing like the store-bought. They made for a fine consolation prize after those long-hoped-for melons rotted before they ripened and the carrots turned out to be riddled with wormholes.

Those onions that we didn't eat right away I braided and hung overhead in the kitchen. It is ridiculously easy to braid onions, and hanging from a hook in the kitchen they add a nice Martha Stewart-like touch. (Once someone asked me if they grew that way, and I said yes.) They kept for several months: longer than the potatoes, which turned green and presumably poisonous within a week of harvesting; longer than the beets and squash, rotting in the fridge; longer than the moldy dried beans.

It seems to me that the onion is the perfect garden vegetable. Onions are food for *people*; they're not caterpillar fodder or raccoon dinner. According to the garden gurus, who recommend growing them as "companion" plants, onions are so disliked by the other animal orders that they can be used as pest repellents.

Onions are never greedy for attention—unlike some vegetables I could mention.

They always look nice, with their neat, soft green tops, and they're edible at every stage—though you don't have to eat them until *you* want to. They are well-connected, too, being near cousins to leeks, garlic, shallots, chives and scallions, which share their virtues. If vegetables got grades, the onion would get straight A's, with special mention for "works and plays well with others."

Does this mean that I will now stop seeking out the bizarre and will devote myself to growing humble crops? Possibly. On the other hand, I've heard of something called the Egyptian onion that makes little bulbs on top of the stalks; it is alleged to be odd-looking though attractive, and a rarity. I could be the first gardener in town to grow them!

ENEMIES LIST

I used to be at peace with nature. An animal-lover, I took my children to the zoo and taught them about our fellow members of the animal kingdom. When they were little, I read *The Tale of Peter Rabbit* to them; we sympathized with the bunnies—Flopsy, Mopsy, Cottontail and Peter—in their struggles against mean old Mr. McGregor, who had already consigned Father Rabbit to the soup pot. Couldn't McGregor see that Peter only wanted a couple of carrots?

Walking in the woods, I treasured the occasional glimpse of deer or raccoon. I used to lose sleep worrying about endangered species; I avoided cosmetics that involved animal testing, and although I never stopped eating meat I felt mildly guilty about it. Swatting the odd mosquito, I wondered whether I was in the right. Someday, I thought, I'd have a garden and be able to grow closer to the wild beings with whom we share our planet.

Then I got my garden and instead of a Peaceable Kingdom I found a battlefield. All creatures great and small were bent upon the undoing of my fledgling garden. Those woodland creatures wanted my flowers! They lusted for my tomatoes—and sharing was

". . . a doe—nervous, and possessing perhaps a more developed sense of shame— will nibble a plant here, snip a shoot there, and then, startled by a falling leaf or something equally perilous to a two-hundred-pound mammal, dash off. . . ."

Michael Pollan
Second Nature

not part of their plan. They weren't about to be propitiated with a few carrots or frightened away by a scarecrow. It was all-out war: my garden and I on one side, with the rest of God's creation ranked against us. I had become Farmer McGregor. This is what gardening does to us; it makes us take the side of the villain in a beloved children's story.

In any war it is necessary to know one's enemies. Beginning with the largest and working down to the microscopic (and skipping over elephants, tigers and bears, although they are probably significant pests in their habitats), we begin with:

DEER

There are two distinctly different ways of looking at deer, depending on whether or not you have them in your garden. To some— the Bambi camp—they are graceful woodland creatures with big startled eyes, cruelly hunted by boorish rifle-toting thugs wearing orange jackets. But to those of us who garden they are greedy predators—"tall rats with hooves," as a friend of mine described them.

I well remember the first time I saw a deer on my property in Fire Island. It was in the early '80s, a spring day. I saw what first seemed to be a large dog, in a thicket of wild cherry trees behind the house: then it moved; I saw the white tuft of tail, a flash of those melting eyes, and it was gone. I was so excited, I called all my friends.

A year or so later those friends and I began to notice that the white-tailed ones were taking an interest in our gardens. At first it seemed sort of charming: "Come look, there's a fawn nibbling on the roses!" One summer there was a huge buck sporting the top half of a bikini on his antlers; he became something of a local hero. But as they got bolder and more numerous, we began to suspect they were out to exterminate our precious little plots. And perhaps us too, as Lyme disease, which is carried by the deer tick, began afflicting the populace.

Through the '80s the talk at every Fire Island gathering—at community meetings, on ferryboats, at "sixish" parties—was about how to keep Bambi out of the yard. Various deterrents were proposed, including commercial animal repellents such as RoPel; they weren't as much fun as the folk remedies. Human hair was one of the first; the reasoning was that the creatures would shy away at the smell. People gathered gleanings from bar-

" 'Deer and ground-hogs love peas . . .' says Kutztown, Pennsylvania, gardener Luther Shaffer. 'Sprinkling dried blood down the rows works to protect the plants. In the garden centers it's very expensive, but at the slaughterhouses it's a by-product that is sold cheaply by the five-gallon can.'

Dried blood has drawbacks, though. If you get heavy rains, you have to reapply, Luther says. 'And it attracts cats.' "

Shelley Goldbloom
Garden Smarts

179

bershop floors and made little hex bags of hair to hang in the trees. Mothballs and perfumed soap had their partisans, too, and some people even talked of buying lion manure from the zoo. Men used the infestation as an excuse to pee off their decks, to "mark" their territory like dogs. Not one of these deterrents worked for more than a few days; dumb as they are, deer aren't *that* dumb.

Some people erected fences, six feet and higher, which the deer leapt over. At various times I tried stringing monofilament fishing line around my garden (the theory was that the animals would get their antlers entangled in the line and go elsewhere; they didn't and they didn't); making scare-deer mobiles out of shiny aluminum pie tins; and building barricades out of brush. The deer got around, or over or even under, everything. One neighbor had planted a peach tree. The first year it produced one peach. Every night my friend wrapped the fruit in aluminum foil; every day she unwrapped it to watch it ripening in the sun. Finally the day approached of the peach's readiness, and my friend put a bottle of champagne on ice. In the morning of the great day she went outside to find the peach discarded on the ground, with big bites torn out of it, the foil tossed aside like a

McDonald's wrapper. Deer don't even have good table manners!

Fire Islanders exchanged lists of plants that the beasts supposedly would not eat. Most of these lists (some of which one finds published in books) are worse than worthless; some of them will say, for example, that deer won't eat thorny plants (after all, *we* don't eat them), when in fact they don't at all mind a few prickles in their salad, and some of their favorite snacks—roses, yucca—have vicious thorns. One book, by Rhonda Massingham Hart, with the perky title *Bugs, Slugs & Other Thugs: Controlling Garden Pests Organically,* has a list that includes such Bambi yummies as tulips, rhododendron and daylilies, as well as yucca; deer will walk through *fire* to get at tulips. (Hart's book, which every time I look at so enrages me I want to pitch it into the compost heap, recommends the usual witchcraft—hair, soap, dirty laundry—and then says: "Don't give up on the usefulness if a particular repellent fails you in one instance." Just keep hanging those bars of soap, while the antlered ones nibble the garden down to bare ground.)

As a hoax, someone wrote a letter to *The Fire Island News* recommending that puma be released on the island as a biological control,

"Conservation laws and hunting customs that concern deer are very strange, anyway. In the absence of wolves and lions, humans are the only predator that could take responsibility for culling herds. But cats and canines kill the weak and the sick, while we by preference kill the very best. To our minds the very best are male. Killing bucks, however, is an ineffective way to decrease deer herds. Whether there are ten bucks or one, all the does in the neighborhood will be impregnated."

Sara Stein
Noah's Garden

181

giving rise to lots of angry and frightened letters from pet owners and parents of small children. At community meetings the gardeners pleaded for a hunting season, outraging the Bambi faction.

Some ten years after my first deer sighting I returned to Fire Island. The big varmints are now so numerous they walk down the streets in broad daylight, mingling with those very same humans of whose hair and soap and urine they were once supposed to be afraid. They knock over garbage cans and eat out of them, perhaps to show their annoyance that no one grows roses for them anymore. There aren't any real gardens now; some people plant a few flowers—marigolds, say, which the deer aren't very fond of—and erect chicken-wire cages around them; this looks about as attractive as it sounds. The latest anti-deer measure involves catching them and—no, *not* butchering them and feeding them to the hungry—injecting them with birth-control hormones.

Not only on Fire Island but all across America, deer populations have increased tremendously in the last fifteen years. There are now more of them (over twenty-five million) than there were before European settlement. But there are also a lot of people. The deer, no fools they, have adapted to changing conditions and become suburbanized. They've learned to overcome their natural timidity; or maybe evolution has dealt with the shy ones. Just as we've learned to prefer *pasta al pesto* over boiled mutton, they've come to like roses.

There are deer nearby, where I live now, but the population is still small, perhaps because of hunting. They are shy and they keep away from human habitations; they might even run away from a handful of hair. But if they ever do start massing in my lettuce patch, I will not waste time on folklore. I'll get either an electric fence or a dog, the only truly effective deterrents. They've driven me from one eden; I won't let it happen again!

What I do have here are:

WOODCHUCKS

Which are also known as groundhogs. This is the beast that crawls out of his hole on February 2 and looks for his shadow. Saint Francis of Assisi would find it difficult to find something nice to say about these creatures. They are ugly and squat with coarse, dirty-looking fur, and they waddle. Gardeners hate them and not just because of their looks: a single woodchuck can eat his way through an entire vegetable garden in a few hours. They don't mind eating flowers, either. They are just about unstoppable. They laugh at fences, or they would if they had any higher senses—such as a sense of humor.

I once watched horrified as a person I knew—a mild-tempered, literary type of person—stoned a woodchuck to death. The animal had got into the garden, fence notwithstanding, and was munching his way through the little vegetable plants, up one

"The first challenge to one's romance with animals comes in April, after you've broken your back turning the soil, humped bales of peat moss and bags of manure from the car trunk to the garden, dug these in by pitchfork, and then laid out in scrupulous rows the seedlings of early crops— lettuce, broccoli, cabbage . . . see how you feel the next morning when this orderly parade ground of seedlings has been mowed down by a woodchuck out snacking."

Michael Pollan
Second Nature

row and down the next. The man shouted at it, shook sticks at it, stamped his feet, used foul language, all to no avail. He threw a pebble, then a little stone, then bigger stones. Finally, still chewing, the creature expired. I never felt quite the same about this person (to whom I was then married), although I've come to understand that woodchucks do push people to extremes.

Here's Michael Pollan, author of *Second Nature* (presumably another mild-tempered, literary sort), scraping road-kill woodchuck off the highway and stuffing it into a burrow. Having read that the animal likes to keep a tidy lair, he hoped to so offend it that it would decide to go live somewhere else. Hah! "In two days' time he had dug a detour around the corpse and the pillaging continued."

Following that same principle, I used to empty the cat litter box into the burrows; gratifying for me, unnoticed by the chuck. Then I bought one of those gas bombs they sell in hardware stores; you light it, throw it deep into the tunnel, and then block the entrance with rocks, trapping the critters inside. It happened to be Good Friday that day, and I speculated that it would be —odd—if I were to come back and find the stones rolled away . . . And lo and behold, it did come to pass that the stones were rolled away, and the varmints lived to munch another day.

In these parts, people talk about wood-chucks the way Fire Islanders talk about deer. "Did you hear what happened to Bob? Whole garden wiped out." No need to name the villain; everyone knows. Build a fence and guys stand around and say: "You don't think they'll get through that?"

Sooner or later guns come up. I couldn't imagine owning one, so I hired a hit man. His name was Ray Krumenacker and he was building a stone wall for us. His gun (rifle, firearm, whatever—*piece*) was a formidable thing with scopes, like something you'd use for a political assassination. Ray himself was rather formidable, stripped to the waist (he's a body builder as well as a stone mason), toting his weapon. It was strange to look up from my desk and see this escapee from a Rambo movie stalking the land. Effective, though: he fired nineteen shots and killed nineteen wood-chucks in five weeks.

Raccoons, etc.

Deer and woodchucks aren't the only fauna amidst the flora. There are more pests out there than most gardeners ever get to shake a stick—or a rifle—at. Many of

"A member of the panel of the BBC's admirable Garden-er's Question Time programme, speaking of identify-ing small creatures in the garden, said that as a lad he was told: 'If it moves slowly enough, step on it; if it doesn't, leave it—it'll prob-ably kill something else.'"

Maureen and
Bridget Boland
Old Wives' Lore for
Gardeners

them, like criminals everywhere, are nocturnal in their habits; our first inkling that raccoons are in the neighborhood may come when we discover the corn stalks stripped of their about-to-be-ripe fruit. The only defense against these intrepid predators is an electric fence—and raccoons are so smart I wouldn't be surprised to hear of one figuring out how to switch off the current.

Porcupines also love corn; and melons and berries—all kinds of fruit; and, as a change of pace, tree bark. Squirrels dig up newly planted bulbs; they're attracted by the smell of fresh earth. They don't eat them, they just bury them somewhere else, and since they refuse to follow the directions—"Plant tulips 6-8 inches deep, root end down, in soil mixed with bone meal"—it's unlikely you'll ever see any results. They, and chipmunks too, like to dig up young seedlings just for the hell of it.

Then there are the tunnelers, the guerrilla warriors of the animal kingdom: chipmunks, gophers and moles, digging under the ground, eating everything they can get their tiny paws on. Mole tunnels can turn your lawn into a broken ankle about to happen. Vole damage, on the other hand, is visible on the *surface* of the grass; you may never actually see a vole,

". . . a complex new order of ecological conflict is playing itself out. At the struggle's center is a hardy opportunistic group of native North American species with both the intelligence to adapt quickly to suburban surroundings and the eclectic appetite to take advantage of

but you can't miss those ugly tracks.

Mice and rats and voles get into your flower beds in the winter and nibble on the roots of your favorite perennials; for dessert they eat the bark off your young fruit trees; then, as a midnight snack (the voles have gone home by now), they'll gnaw their way into the potting shed, and open up all the bags and boxes of expensive stuff you've been saving, and polish off whatever seems good: grass seed, rubber boots, dahlia tubers, catalogs, burlap, garden gloves, superphosphate. These verminous critters are *omnivores.*

Then there's the opossum: uglier than a woodchuck, smart as a raccoon, meaner than a rat and almost as undiscriminating; the best thing I know about these beasts is that they are fairly uncommon.

Unlike rabbits, which are everywhere. Rabbits are so cute, one would be happy to have a few of them as garden pets if only they weren't so greedy. Give Flopsy a lettuce leaf and she'll eat the whole garden, and then— quick as a bunny!—drop a new litter of bunnies. One female can produce six litters of eight rabbit kittens a year, with each of those infants attaining sexual maturity in just a few months . . .

the wide variety of foods that suburbanites wittingly and unwittingly serve up. Crow and blue jay, mallard duck and Canada goose; squirrel, cottontail, skunk and white-tailed deer . . . are emerging as winners in give-no-quarter combat with a much larger number of more sensitive and less adaptable species that include many songbirds and uncommon plants."

William K. Stevens, in The New York Times, March 1, 1994

What is one to do? Other than deer—which are protected—it is legal to kill varmints on your own property. But it's hard to do if you're a lily-livered, urban-born wimp like me. I couldn't take a dead 'possum out of a trap. (Dealing with the cats' discarded mice is bad enough.)

Live trapping is the solution commonly recommended. You can buy a gadget called a Havahart, which will catch your beast without hurting it; then you release it. But where? I can see how this would be a good idea if one had a real enemy—a human enemy, that is, like an ex-spouse. It might be amusing to drop a raccoon or a family of rabbits on an enemy's lawn, but failing that, what do you do with them? And what if they come back? I know one couple who trapped a woodchuck that had been eating their garden, injuring the creature's nose slightly in the process. They drove the chuck in his cage to a wildlife preserve five miles away and released it, only to have the same animal, scarred nose and all, turn up in their garden a few days later!

It turns out that taking wild animals from place to place is actually illegal in some states, which is a sensible law. Moving wild—and possibly rabid—animals around strikes me as an extremely silly and unwise thing to do, and probably not very kind to the animal in question. There are even people who take great pains to catch house mice alive to then release out of doors, whereupon the mice either quickly run back to the house or slowly die.

If you don't want to kill anything yourself, you might enlist some animal predators. Cats can be (if they want to be) effective against vermin up to the size of a large rabbit; a big barky dog will deal with just about anything. "Good" wild animals are said to include foxes, snakes, shrews, bats, owls, coyotes, weasels, and even such fearsome beasts as wolves and pumas; but how one might encourage them I do not know, nor do I want to find out.

More and more, barriers such as fences— sturdy, tall electrified fences, with anti-tunneling extensions underground—turn out to be the only recourse. As the wild herbivores gain in number, the stalag look spreads through American gardens. This summer, when a wood-chuck began using my pumpkin field as a salad bar, I found myself wondering if I could rig up something with razor wire.

Not even the best fence is protection against aerial attack. Some of our worst predators are:

"No one around here puts up scarecrows anymore. The birds in this neighborhood have become so accustomed to humans that they scarcely shy in the presence of real people, let alone fake ones."

Roger B. Swain
The Practical
Gardener

BIRDS

Beautiful to look at and listen to, harbingers of spring, symbols of freedom, exemplars of domestic virtue: everyone loves birds. But why are they eating the cherries?

On closer study they turn out to have a lot of faults, and bad habits. In fact, there are good birds—bluebirds, wrens, robins, song sparrows—and bad birds. And the bad ones—starlings, house sparrows—not only closely resemble the good ones, but they have muscled their way into the bluebird house (which you built yourself from a kit), where they are breeding *more* nasty little birds and making a horrid racket in the process. And once these feathered fiends grow up, they'll fly directly to your berry patch.

Then there are the true criminals: the crows and jays and—oh horrors—Canada geese. These last were once, and not very long ago, beloved visitors. There would come a moment, late in summer, when you'd hear the rich, resonant music of their honking: you'd look up to see that long, ragged vee. "Autumn's coming," you'd say, "the wild geese are flying south." Wild no longer. Flying south no more. Like the deer, they've adapted to suburban life, fig-

ured out that it's easier to hang around farm ponds and village greens and freeload, than to make that long trip twice a year. Vast flocks of these enormous birds have taken over parks in the Northeast, eating everything in sight, leaving masses of their signature cigar-shaped droppings.

Even the sainted robin is not above stealing a blueberry here, a cherry there, and while on grub and bug patrol in the yard, if he comes across a precious earthworm he'll gobble it up without a second thought.

So what's to be done? Mostly, *nothing.*

You could construct a scarecrow; this would make a nice creative project, but no one, not even the most starry-eyed folk wisdom advocates, claims that they are effective. Other scare tactics: rubber snakes and owls, fake cats, real cats, noisemakers (pinwheels, flapping streamers, radios tuned to Rush Limbaugh), sprinklers set to go on every hour, etc., may be effective *for a while*; until the birds figure them out. This may or may not give you time to harvest the corn. Barrier methods once again are the best solution, though draping netting over a row of blueberry bushes, or an orchard of cherry trees, isn't my idea of easy.

Live and let live is the best—maybe the only—policy with birds. Think of the lost berries and earthworms as fair recompense for the pleasure they bring and the work they do; and hope they don't take a mind to dig up all your freshly planted seeds. If you've the stomach for it, killing starlings is legal. As for those Canada geese: they probably won't bother you unless you have a large pond. If they do, you could always move. Or you could console yourself with the knowledge that they eat slugs.

"A direct hit with fresh lime juice kills [slugs], as does a concoction called 'slug juice.' This is made by putting the remains of a cup or two of dead slugs into a blender, pureeing them, and then straining the resulting mush.

Hair can also be used to kill snails. By snipping coarse hair, such as human or horse hair, into tiny pieces and scattering it in areas frequented by snails, you can eliminate them. Tiny hairs irritate the soft moist skin of the snail and he dehydrates himself to death in his effort to expel the irritating hairs clinging to him."

Rhonda Massingham
Hart
Bugs, Slugs &
Other Thugs

LOWEST OF THE LOW

It is hard to know what God had in mind when he created slugs. I shall never forget my first sighting of a California banana slug. It was in the early '60s. I opened the back door of my San Francisco flat and there was this—thing, the size and shape of a banana, wet and slimy and sort of quivering all over . . . Was it a hallucination? Had I overindulged the night before? I slammed the door and stayed inside until some native Californian came along to tell me what it was.

We don't have banana slugs here in the East, although the local variety can get to be several inches long. (There are also snails, which are slugs that at least have the decency to cover their disgusting bodies. They are more common in Europe, where they are known as escargots.)

Summers when we don't have a drought, we get slugs. They take little bites out of ripe fruit—tomatoes, squash, strawberries. They eat holes in lettuce and cabbage leaves, and consume entire plantings of young seedlings; they are especially fond of delphiniums and marigolds and hosta.

One looks to the garden mavens for practical advice on getting rid of the loathsome ones, and what do you get? You certainly don't get a good night's sleep.

"Prowl for slugs with a flashlight at night, and check their hiding places (under rocks and boards, for example) by day" (Barbara Damrosch, *The Garden Primer*). Go on a "predawn flashlight raid—handpicking the offenders and dropping them into a pail of salted water to finish them off while they're still groggy" (Hart, *Bugs, Slugs & Other Thugs*). One popular slug-trap involves saucers of beer, strategically placed about the garden. Then there are methods that take advantage of the supposed delicacy of the slugs' tummies: crushed limestone or pieces of window screen laid on the ground or cut up to make little fences. Hart suggests sheets of copper: "Since copper carries a weak electric current, slimy slugs and snails really get a charge out of it."

I have my doubts about the tender tummy theory. My Fire Island garden was full of slugs. One year I cut up window screening into narrow strips and fashioned dozens of little collars, which I carefully placed around each little marigold plant. It looked ridiculous, but at least my flowers were safe, I thought; a few days later, missing buds and that familiar slime trail showed me that I was wrong. Did they climb the little fences? Leap? Stand on each other's shoulders? I shall never know. Not long afterward I abandoned that garden and moved to upstate New York, where a new community of slugs soon found me.

What is one to do? I refuse to leave my warm cozy bed in the middle of the night to go slug-hunting. There are chemical baits, of course, but they're highly toxic; one worries about pets. Beer is too good for slugs, I think, and emptying a saucer of beer-and-dead slug soup takes a stronger stomach than I'll ever have.

What I like to do with slugs is salt them—in the daytime, by the light of the sun. They die quickly and there is no mess to dispose of. (Of course, one has to take care not to get a lot of salt on the plants.) True, the method is labor-intensive, but I find the job satisfaction is high—and it's as effective as any other system.

THE LITTLE GUYS

The bad news: "Eighty percent of all animals on this planet are insects of the order Arthropoda" (*The Wise Garden Encyclopedia*). The really bad news: "There are a million species described in scientific literature, and entomologists estimate only ten percent are known." We are hopelessly outnumbered, surrounded by infinite hordes of infinitesimal beasties. It's enough to make one think fondly of bunnies and deer, even Canada geese. (But not of slugs.)

Some of those ten percent are all too well known. Consider the cutworm: "Fat, 1" long, gray or black segmented larvae" (*Rodale's All-New Encyclopedia of Organic Gardening*). This icky creature lives under the ground, lying in wait for tender seedlings, which he cruelly decapitates. A solitary fellow, he does his dirty work at night. Unlike the Japanese beetle: these flying monsters can often be found in clusters, partying in the raspberry patch. They are fond of beans and roses and many ornamentals, and in their larval stage wreak all kinds of havoc under the ground.

Plagues of insects have been known since biblical times; our locusts and grasshoppers are proud to be part of a grand old tradition. Some of the other bugs munching and slurping away out there are: mealybugs, borers, whiteflies, weevils, earwigs, thrips, leafhoppers and maggots. Scales have shells, like tiny turtles; they cling to bark and, as they feed, inject toxins that gradually kill the tree. Spittlebugs lay their eggs in grass, in what looks like a clump of spit; when they grow up, they hop around the garden sampling little bites of whatever takes their fancy. Aphids are tiny and translucent—and ubiquitous. They suck the sap out of the tenderest part of the plant (rosebuds are a particular favorite), weakening the host so that other pests and diseases can gain admittance.

Caterpillars are masters of disguise: in some cases they take on the color of whatever they're grazing on—pink ones on the petunias, yellow on the mums. Some of them are adorable fluffy little things, like tiny Persian kittens. To swat or not to swat? Unless one is an entomologist it's hard to know whether a given crawler is a good guy—perhaps an incipient fritillary—or a villain. Many of them effect dramatic Jekyll-Hyde transformations: those pretty little white butterflies dancing in the air in June will soon produce voracious cabbage worms. The beautiful swallowtail butterfly spends half his existence as a parsley worm, chomping his way through the herb garden. At least with the gypsy moth you know where you stand; even in the adult stage, he's an ugly-looking beast. In the larval form they turn into those infamous caterpillars that periodically lay waste to our gardens, consuming every leaf on every tree in a matter of weeks.

The only thing worse than an organism attacking your garden is a microorganism. Nematodes, viruses, bacteria and spores are out there in vast numbers, a deadly, invisible army. They can't be seen, but the diseases they cause—the blights, rots, cankers, wilts, mildews, galls, rusts, curls and smuts—are all too visible. And all too often, by the time the damage is evident, the plant is past saving.

Quick, the Flit!

For most of history, mankind had few weapons with which to battle the insect kingdom: smudge pots in orchards, poisons such as arsenic and lead, flyswatters, sacrifices to the gods; it wasn't much of an arsenal. Then came DDT.

DDT was first used widely during the Second World War, when it was found to be highly effective against the mosquitoes that cause malaria. Farmers and home gardeners soon embraced it, as well as the other synthetic pesticides that quickly came on the

"Spraying for mosquito control in areas of heavy population also kills a wide range of insects that attack cultivated plants. Many gardeners can now grow broccoli, cabbage, and other members of the cabbage family without spraying or dusting because chemicals that control the mosquitoes also kill the fat green larvae of the cabbage butterfly.

Beetles are hard to kill with direct sprays, but most broad-spectrum insecticides contain at least one chemical to which they are sensitive. When in doubt, use DDT."

The American Home Garden Book and Plant Encyclopedia, *1963* market. They were easy to use, quick and effective, and they were safe; or so they seemed at the time. The pesticides, along with the new chemical fertilizers, precipitated the so-called Green Revolution. For the first time gardeners had the upper hand; it seemed as though the entire planet would soon be made to yield food crops. Man's long battle with nature was won!

It must have been wonderful, a modern Golden Age, that brief era between the invention of DDT and the grim discovery that it caused far worse problems than it cured. In 1962 Rachel Carson's book *Silent Spring* spelled out the deadly truth about the wonderful chemical insecticides, and in 1973 DDT was banned. Since then, one pesticide after another has been found to be hazardous.

There are still plenty of chemicals on the market, of course. About midway through every summer I find myself browsing through the pesticides at the local Agway. Usually it's the Japanese beetles on the roses that bring me to this pass. I'd never use chemicals on a food crop, but since I don't eat roses (unlike just about every other living thing) why *not* spray them? This is my reasoning. But I usually go home empty-handed after reading the

". . . we want to call the home gardener's attention to the recently developed all-purpose remedies for insect control, and to mention especially the preparation known as Malathion, which has been thoroughly tested by the United States Department of Agriculture and released for home gardening use. Malathion is especially effective as an insecticide for vegetable gardens and for fruit crops."

Albert E. Wilkinson and Victor A. Tiedjens, The Handy Book of Gardening, *1950*

197

"Although Bt is natural in that it has a biological origin, it's questionable whether spraying is a natural use of it. It is not an infectious organism, not a caterpillar disease. It is a soil organism, a decayer, that has no known relationship with insects. . . . one must ask, is the meeting of a soil spore with a gypsy moth caterpillar on an oak leaf natural? And is the death itself—a case of mistaken identity, a protein fragment grasped in good faith because it is similar to one that gut cells ordinarily welcome —a natural event?"

Sara Stein
Noah's Garden

warnings: "Causes irreversible eye damage" (Bonide Rose and Flower Spray or Dust). Not *might* cause or *can* cause: "causes"! No thanks.

Of late even farmers—who traditionally will risk anything to get a harvest—have turned against chemicals. The USDA no longer recommends them as a universal panacea; not because of their toxicity to people or birds, not because of their impact upon the future of the planet, but because they *don't work.*

The bugs have become resistant to the poisons. Broad-spectrum pesticides turn out to be as fallible as broad-spectrum antibiotics: just as germs have learned to live with penicillin, evolving into tough and deadly warriors, insects and microorganisms have adapted to the chemical challenge. So much for better living through chemistry.

GREENER THAN THOU

Most gardeners nowadays call themselves organic, even if it's just for the few weeks in spring between the planting of the first radishes and peas, and the sighting of the first chewed leaf.

What *do* you do about that leaf? Ignore it at first probably, but if it develops into a full-scale infestation, what do you do?

Handpicking of bugs is easy and effective and even fun, once you overcome your squeamishness. This is not a job for the faint-hearted: for those who shriek at the sight of a worm, or who retain any lingering feelings of reverence for life.

Consider the tomato hornworm, my favorite bug: this bizarre-looking beastie betrays his presence by the stripped leaves and the little pellets of doodoo he leaves behind; he hides in the tomato plants, and it can be astonishingly difficult to find him. Once you track him down, it's up to you whether to stomp him or jar him. But wait: are there little white specks clinging to his back? Don't stomp. The cunningly designed hornworm carries his doom on his back. The specks are the eggs of the braconid wasp, soon to turn into larvae that will destroy the tomato worm—in a much more horrible way than you could ever devise— before flying off to do other good works in garden and orchard.

There are worse ways to spend an afternoon than catching Japanese beetles. They're easy to find: they hang out in the roses and the raspberry bushes in clumps of two or three, busily having beetle sex, and being preoccupied they're easily caught. Some people drown them in

"I am no hunter. It doesn't really matter how many legs are involved—two, four, six, eight. I don't even like to kill slugs, and they have no legs at all. A friend fills a pint container with slugs every morning, adds a little water, and brings them to a boil on the stove. I would as soon strangle bunnies."

Roger B. Swain
The Practical
Gardener

jars of vinegar and water, or salt and water; plain water won't do, they swim. I like to squinch them, with or without gloves. (Pinch + squish = squinch.) A few years ago Anne Raver, writing in *The New York Times,* suggested snipping them in half with secaturs. Suggestible fool that I am, I promptly spent an hour unsuccessfully trying to bisect beetles. I finally concluded that the only way to get them to hold still for the procedure would be to dope them—perhaps with a blast of DDT. I went back to squinching. (But cutting in half works on slugs and caterpillars.)

Handpicking, while satisfying, has its limitations. It won't work with very tiny or very lively bugs, or with huge infestations. By the end of July, as wave upon wave of Japanese beetle migration descends upon my property, I need a better means of control. One summer I bought traps. These are yellow plastic gizmos, impregnated with scent that mimics the beetle's own pheromones (it smells like dime-store perfume); expecting a good time, the sex-crazed beetles flock to the traps, where they fall inside and can't get out. One difficulty is that the traps have to be emptied frequently, leaving you with the problem of what to do with all those pheromoned-out beetles. Also, as with any device that works by luring pests, there's a chance that you might be actually *attracting* more troublemakers to the garden than you are exterminating.

In addition to traps and handpicking, the organic gardener's bag of tricks contains hundreds of methods, some practical, some silly, some worse than useless.

GOOD GARDENING. This includes good housekeeping: removing diseased plant matter from the garden; rotation planting (don't grow your tomatoes in the same spot every year, else the same diseases will find them); and keeping the soil chock-full of compost and manure and other expensive nutrients. It's a case of a truckload of prevention instead of a spray can of cure. What this theory also does is make the gardener feel guilty for having problems: if one had only vacuumed up the dead leaves, or added another $100 worth of guano, there might not be so many bugs on the cauliflower.

BARRIERS—collars (made of paper or plastic) that go around seedlings to keep out cutworms. Floating row covers: lightweight, nonwoven cloth, that you lay over newly planted beds, the theory being that they keep

"I have other objections to what is called trap-cropping. . . . I don't see the sense of it, not because it doesn't work but because it does. It is quite true that eggplants next to potatoes will be more attractive to the potato beetle than the potatoes are; that zinnias (especially in white or pale colors), white roses and white geraniums will lure Japanese beetles away from other plants; and that dill charms the tomato hornworms into deserting the tomatoes. What of it? What of the eggplants, zinnias, white roses, dill, I have lost in the process?"

Eleanor Perenyi
Green Thoughts

"Use of 1% rotenone powder to control blowfly infestations had been recommended in the past, but recent research indicates that rotenone powder has very little effect on fly larvae. Unfortunately, rotenone is very effective in eliminating the Nasonia wasp, a tiny parasite which provides natural control of the blowfly larvae. Therefore, we discourage the use of rotenone in nesting boxes."

New York State
Bluebird Society
The Bluebird News

out egg-laying moths and the bugs that prey upon young seedlings. Within limitations—they don't keep out slugs or cutworms, and they must be removed eventually from plants that need pollinating—they are extremely useful. They do not add to the good looks of the garden.

COMPANION PLANTING—growing plants in combinations that may (or may not) have an effect upon pest populations. Garlic and onions are alleged insect deterrents. I grow garlic chives among my roses. (They produce pretty white flowers in August.) I still have aphids and beetles and all the other problems that roses are heir to, but conceivably it would be worse without the chives.

Marigolds are often planted to repel nematodes; of course, marigolds are catnip to slugs. Will the slugs stay on the marigolds and ignore the lettuce? The Rodale encyclopedia advises us to "plant dill near your tomatoes. It attracts hornworms, and they're easier to spot on dill than they are on tomato plants." But why would I want to attract them in the first place? Isn't this a case of borrowing trouble?

HOME BREWS—those soups and teas you whip up in your blender, containing the usual ingredients: wormwood, garlic, hot peppers, ashes, banana skins, baking soda; eye of newt, toe of caterpillar . . .

ORGANIC INSECTICIDES. A wide array of "earth-friendly" products are on the market; this is a burgeoning business! There are soaps and oils, which are reasonably safe to use; they are effective if you keep at it—and keep at it . . . Copper and sulfur are naturally occurring minerals that have been used as fungicides for centuries. (Which doesn't mean that they aren't poisonous.) Botanicals—substances from plants—include pyrethrin (from daisies), rotenone, sabadilla, ryania, neem, etc. Many of these are toxic to mammals; none of them is guaranteed not to kill desirable insects, such as butterflies, bees and ladybugs. The difference between them and the egregious chemicals is that they don't linger in the environment—so far as one knows. Hardline greens—such as the people at *Organic Gardening*—disapprove of them.

GOOD BUGS. Yes, there are such things. Ladybugs, praying mantises, soldier bugs, various wasps (including the one that cannibalizes the tomato worm), beneficial nematodes, etc. The list is long and growing longer. You can buy these little warriors (giftwrapped) or kits to lure them into your yard. Insects don't always take kindly to relocation, so don't be too surprised if your ladybugs promptly fly away home.

The organic purists don't like to buy anything. Rather than send away to, say, "Gardens Alive," for a few thousand green lacewing larvae or trichogramma wasps, they will plant specific crops—among them dandelion and Queen Anne's lace—that presumably attract beneficial bugs to the garden. (Now that you know

THE GARDENER'S GRIPE BOOK

about this, you too can pretend that the weeds in your garden are there on purpose.)

GOOD DISEASES. Milky spore disease is bacteria that kill the grubs of the Japanese beetle. It's expensive; it would cost a fortune to dose my entire property, and it might be several years before the effect was felt—if it worked at all. Bt—Bacillus thuringiensis—is a natural toxin, which has been effective against the dread gypsy moth, among others.

At first heralded as the organic gardener's answer to problem pests, some of these forms of germ warfare have been found, at second glance, to be problematic. Milky spore disease kills good grubs (even grubs can be good!) as well as bad. Bt, which has been widely used for only a few years, has already engendered resistant bugs. Some pests—such as the Indian mealmoth—have figured it out in only a couple of generations.

In order that Bt not lose its effectiveness, farmers are now being advised to "keep a part of their crops untreated so the insect pest can thrive there. The idea is to keep susceptible individuals alive and prevent the population from being dominated by resistant insects" (William K. Stevens, *The New York Times,* December 29, 1992). In other words, maintain

"There is nothing more unpleasant than to tell anyone suffering under a calamity that there is no tangible remedy; but it is infinitely better to do so than to delude them with a false one. I have been a worker of the soil since my boyhood, and every year's experience convinces me of the helplessness of remedies against insects or other blighting

an area of your garden—in addition to the section you've set aside for bugs and weeds—as a wildlife preserve for insects that aren't resistant to Bt, which can then be released in the cabbage patch, there to be killed by Bt.

IPM

It's August, the Japanese beetles are camped out on the roses; also on the beans and the zinnias. It is not a pretty sight. The milky spore disease I scattered on the lawn two years ago has had no effect as yet. I've given up on traps, I'm burned out on squinching. I've squirted Safer's insecticidal soap, dusted with rotenone, then with pyrethrin. Irreversible eye damage no longer seems such a threat; what's the use of having eyes if all I can see is beetles? My hand closes on the spray can . . .

This process, whereby one begins with the most benign organic controls and winds up using malathion, is known as IPM (Integrated Pest Management). It was developed for commercial growers as a way of managing pests with the least possible chemical interference. It is frowned upon by the strictly organic contingent, and with reason. What seems at first to be sensible and pragmatic is, in fact, just a means of justifying the use of

plagues that attack vegetation in the open field. It is true that the amateur gardener may save his dozen or two of cabbages or roses by daily picking off or destroying the insects; but when it comes to broad acres, I much doubt if ever any remedy will be found to be practicable."

Peter Henderson,
Gardening for Profit,
1874

chemicals. "I tried to reason with them, Your Honor, but they wouldn't listen so I whacked them."

I don't like agreeing with the organic purists because I so often find them insufferable. I am offended by their insistence that pests and diseases exclusively afflict unhealthy gardens; blaming the victim, I call this. Bad things *do* happen to good gardeners. I resent their blithe assurance that the Japanese beetles will go away if I "Shake beetles from plants in early morning; apply floating row covers; set out baited traps throughout community; apply milky disease spores to soil. . . ." (Rodale). I would prefer to be told the truth, which is: If I want to garden, I'm going to have pests.

MOTHBALLS & SNAKES

F olk wisdom—the kind passed over whatever is the current equivalent of the back fence—is full of uses for mothballs, which is curious when you think that mothballs are actually little round balls of poison. But they are perennially popular in household remedies, perhaps because they are old-fashioned; Granny kept a box of them under the sink.

I first heard of using mothballs in the garden a few years ago, when the deer began munching on my garden in Fire Island. The advice then current was to sprinkle mothballs on the soil, in between the deer's—and my—favorite plants, such as the rosebushes, and to tuck them in the ground when planting bulbs. I can't remember the original source of the advice; it traveled by word of mouth from one gardener to the next, and I'm undoubtedly guilty of passing it along myself.

In due time our Fire Island hamlet smelled like a clothes closet. The deer didn't seem to mind the smell, nor did it deter the little varmints who dig up tulip bulbs. The fact that it's ineffective is, of course, no reason to stop using a home remedy. If the deer grazed on the roses, or the bulbs failed to come up, we told ourselves that

*A narrow Fellow in
the Grass
Occasionally rides—
. . .*

*Several of Nature's
People
I know, and they
know me—
I feel for them a
transport
Of cordiality—*

*But never met this
Fellow
Attended, or alone
Without a tighter
breathing
And Zero at the
Bone—*

Emily Dickinson,
"A Narrow Fellow in
the Grass"

we hadn't used enough mothballs, or the rain had washed them away. Mothballs are cheap, so we bought more and more of them. I stuck them in with the impatiens seedlings in New York, to foil the squirrels. And when I moved my gardening efforts to the country, I kept on religiously planting mothballs. I'd probably still be doing it, if not for the snakes.

One is supposed to like snakes, I know; they eat little garden pests like mice and grasshoppers. As the enemy of my enemies, they should be counted among my friends. I don't care for them, though—they give me the creeps. There is a planting of evergreen shrubs in front of our house that is home to a tribe of garter snakes, and this is too close for my comfort. I don't like to have a snake looking at me through the window, or to contemplate the next stage: that he might decide to join me in the living room.

No one will tell you how to get rid of snakes; perhaps—short of getting a mongoose—there is no way of eliminating them. Look in the index of any garden book under Snakes and what do you see? "Snakes, as beneficial animals" (*Rodale's All-New Encyclopedia*). No entry at all for "Snakes, how to get rid of."

I was happy, then, to find in the household hint column in a newspaper the suggestion that my old friend the mothball would repel the slithery ones. I immediately bought a carton of mothballs and sprinkled the contents liberally about the shrubs in front of the house.

The very next day I saw, through the dining room windows, two big garter snakes festooned along the branches of a dwarf blue spruce, basking in the warm sunshine, close enough to the mothballs to make it very clear that they didn't mind the smell at all. If it's possible for a snake to smile, those two were

". . . if I had a natural lawn, especially in the West, I would be watching for something else: snakes. That I am dealing with a grass snake or a king cobra makes no difference to me, and the mere possibility that one was lurking in my natural lawn would be enough to make me cut it down and return to the tiresome disciplines of turf."

Eleanor Perenyi
Green Thoughts

beaming. At that moment my simple trusting faith in mothballs was shattered forever. I don't even use them in the closets anymore.

As for the snakes, I'm trying to overcome my fear of them, so far with moderate success. I bought a big rubber snake at a toy store, and I move it from place to place about the house, hoping that familiarity will desensitize me. The program is working to the extent that I'm no longer afraid of rubber snakes. Not very.

THE WISH BOOKS

Winter, for those gardeners who have it, is the best season of all. Even if you neglected to turn the compost heap one last time before it froze, and if you didn't fasten styrofoam cones around the roses (although you remembered to *buy* the cones) or get around to heaping six to eight inches of mulch around the tender little feet of those precious shrubs you put in last year, or plow a truckload of manure into the vegetable plot—if you simply walked away from the garden after the first frost, leaving the blackened plants to stand where they died—by Christmas it's too late to do anything about anything.

Unless you have the misfortune to live in a frost-free climate (year-round weeding!), this is the one time of the year when the garden doesn't cry out for help. The pests are gone, dead of cold or, more likely, lurking in their cocoons and underground burrows. It no longer matters that the apple trees produced no apples this year, that the roses had more insects than blooms, or that your neighbor's tomatoes were earlier, juicier and tastier than yours. The winds blow, it snows or it doesn't snow, and the gardener sits inside, content to leave matters to Mother Nature and Father Time, that swell couple.

Oh, if you had to, you suppose, you could put on your boots and all your woollies and go out there and hack away at the underbrush; and if you were truly compulsive you could sharpen your tools and oil them, and take the lawn mower in to the shop for a tune-up, but day length alone limits these projects. Anyway, the gardener's true winter work is indoors: winter is catalog season.

JANUARY JOYS

Those catalogs start turning up in my mailbox around Thanksgiving, but I refuse to look at them until January. It takes me that long to get into the right frame of mind. If I had to face spring catalogs in November, I might just give up the whole enterprise; sell the farm and move to a high-rise condo in Florida and grow plastic palms on the balcony.

But by January all is forgiven. Last summer's garden is a distant memory, its tribulations and tragedies forgotten. As with childbirth, you've forgotten the pain and aggravation and you're ready to start again. The Japanese beetles no longer seem like an invincible army; you're willing to believe that some strategically placed traps will deal with them. Forgetting that you've never been able to grow a cantaloupe that was bigger or sweeter than a turnip, you imagine a field full of the ambrosial French Charentais melons, with maybe a corner set aside for some heirloom honeydews. There you sit dreaming, and here come the wishbooks to sell you all those seeds and plants and Japanese beetle traps, and more; they're ready to provide you with things you didn't even known you wanted. Get a good blaze going in the fireplace, pull up a chair—it's catalog time!

By January the catalog stack is a small mountain, full of duplicates. Some companies keep up a steady bombardment, sending out identical offerings weekly, disguised with different glossy covers. Some sellers mail them out two or three at a clip, perhaps believing that the sheer mass of paper will persuade the reader that their offerings are superior. (As someone who lives in an area without garbage collection, where trash must be hauled to the dump, I'm not won over by this tactic.)

There are *catalogues*: slick magazine-like books, with drop-dead gorgeous art and fancy text, that would be at home on a coffee table; and there are plain old *catalogs,* with straightforward photos of cabbages and marigolds and beans, printed on coated newsprint like super-

"January is traditionally the month to pore over seed catalogues. If you wait until February, you're already behind, because you should be starting your leeks, under lights, along with two billion viola seeds. When nongardeners say 'I guess it's pretty quiet in the garden right now,' I laugh hysterically."

Anne Raver, in
The New York Times,
January 8, 1995

213

market tabloids. There are black-and-white pamphlets on recycled paper, printed in soybean ink that look to be, and perhaps are, stapled together in someone's kitchen; and some of these are so full of New Age lore and admonishments about the environment, you might almost lose sight of the fact that they too are catalogs. Some of the most esoteric don't even have illustrations, assuming that all their customers will know what Lollo Rossa lettuce and *Blanc double de Coubert* roses look like.

After discarding all the duplicates, I sort through what's left, cataloging the catalogs: Tried-and-true; Tried-and-found-wanting; Untried-but-attractive; and You-never-know. I leaf through the more appealing, sticking Post-it notes here and there, underlining possible selections, dog-earing the pages. A dream garden gradually emerges out of the flames in the fireplace, full of brilliantly colored flowers, fragrant herbs, succulent fruit.

There are all those *New!* (nothing is ever just plain new) plant varieties, products of the hybridizers and genetic tinkerers. Some flowers—marigolds, for example—seem to be totally redesigned every few years, like women's fashions. There are also rediscovered heirlooms for the nostalgic among us, and this season's odd-tasting salad green for the adventurous (last year's was tatsoi). And there are the old friends, the plants I grow every year, some of which, like petunias, disappoint on an annual basis. But in the glow of my January reverie I'm convinced this summer will be different . . .

Suddenly I awake with a start: it's almost February and I haven't ordered anything! It's already too late to cash in on some of the giveaway offers. It's time to stop mooning over those alluring pictures and get real.

HITTING THE BOOKS

All at once one is faced with a blizzard of small print, much of which seems to be in code. There are cryptic initials, Latin terms, jargon. What is a *tetraploid*? What does "Grow as annual" mean? "Tender perennial"? How can a plant be "half-hardy"? There's text and there's subtext: is "vigorous" a euphemism for "invasive"? Do the words "flamboyant" and "stunning" really mean "loud" and "vulgar"? Did the copywriter's failure to mention flavor mean that this particular tomato has none? If all the other eggplants boast of their resistance to something called verticillium wilt, does that mean this one may succumb to it?

Even the photographs are open to question. That blue impatiens: can that color actually exist in nature? All those immaculately clean leeks, glistening melon slices, artfully arranged peppers, bug-free cabbages—are they *for real*?

Jumping back and forth among catalogs, one begins to notice discrepancies, contradictions. How come White Flower Farm describes *Rosa celsiana* as having repeat bloom—when Roses of Yesterday and Today says it blooms only once a summer? (White Flower is wrong.) Cultural instructions for the same plant

"The major trend this year is . . . toward fussing up and multiplying the number of petals by one means or another. If there is a flower with individuality and a set of delicate single petals, the horticulturists seem determined to double or triple them, to curl them, ruffle them, and inevitably to make them bigger. . . . all blossom form seems to be disappearing, causing one to look fearfully ahead to the time when our garden beds will be full of great shaggy heads, alike except for color, all just great blobs of bloom."

Katharine S. White,
Onward and Upward
in the Garden,
1959

215

". . . I have never seen the term 'invasive' in a seed catalogue, but I know very few gardeners who haven't spent endless hours on their knees grubbing out buttercups or trying to halt the forward progress of the lamb's ear."

Cass Peterson, in
The New York Times,
November 29, 1992

can vary from catalog to catalog. Want to grow morning glories? According to Park Seed it's a cinch: "Easily grown in sun in even the poorest soils. . . . Sow outdoors where wanted." But Thompson & Morgan sings a different tune: "Sow early; Germ 1-3 weeks 75F; after 14 days chip ungerminated seeds."

On the other hand, there are some weird similarities among the different catalog companies. That little girl in the sunflower patch: haven't I seen her before? Sure enough, the same child—red shirt, blue jumper, brown hair, bangs—appears in Burpee's, Park's, Gurney's and Henry Field's catalogs (and perhaps in some others), always in ads for a misbegotten variety of sunflower called "Sunspot," whose claim to fame is that, although it has dinner plate-size flowers, the stems are only eighteen inches tall. My suspicions aroused, I rummage around and find some old catalogs from previous seasons; she's in them too! For all I know, her picture has been running in seed catalogs for decades. The little girl could be grown by now—tall enough to appear in ads for full-size sunflowers.

My particular bête-noire is the indexes. I would like to pass a law that all plant and seed purveyors must use standardized indexes and, even more important, run them in the *same place* in the catalog: inside the front cover, say, or in the centerfold. Anyone who has ever spent an hour rummaging through seventeen catalogs looking for Cranberry beans or Blue Ballet squash or Silver salvia, will agree that this is a major annoyance.

There are Issues: "treated" seed is one. This is seed that's been dusted with a fungicide so it won't rot, or whatever. Is this a necessary evil—or a monstrous crime against the environment? The more organic catalog companies eschew treated seed. Some companies treat seed without telling so (except in small print on some page of the catalog that you're unlikely to see); and some companies ride both sides of the fence, which is really confusing.

The open-pollinated versus hybrid issue is another question that, if gardeners engaged in physical violence instead of putting all their energy into digging holes, would lead to bloodshed. To an ordinary grower, hybrids—bred to be better or bigger or to have greater disease resistance—would seem superior. But for an environmentalist, growing old-time plant varieties—the heliotropes Granny grew, the limas that Thomas Jefferson's kids refused to eat—is a sacred task, a way of ensuring that the genetic material stored in the seed will survive. It's bad enough to have to choose among so many offerings: now we're supposed to decide matters of global significance!

HARD CHOICES

Pencil in hand, I begin. This is when I start saying over and over again like a mantra: *Everything you buy—every seed, every plant, every bulb—means a hole that must be dug.* If I ordered everything that attracted me, I'd wind up with enough plants to fill this county—

"There is no question that old-fashioned, heirloom flowers and vegetables have an appealing quaintness that is in sync with the back-to-basics zeitgeist: 'Save the 100-year-old egg-plant!' However, any astute gardener will tell you that the benefits of a modern hybrid over an older variety are like those of a new car over a 1918 Model T. It might look nice in your garden but you wouldn't want to drive it across the country."

George Ball, Jr., chairman of W. Atlee Burpee & Company, in a New York Times op-ed piece

although it would still be only a tiny fraction of what's available. Keeping a clear mental picture of all those holes, and of myself digging them, I start making choices. It should be fairly simple—a matter of picking the best seeds or plants, at the best price, and ordering them.

It is not easy. In fact, as hard work goes it's as arduous as any outdoor task.

Relative prices aren't always easy to judge. If I wanted to grow the grotesque Sunspot sunflower, which I do not, Henry Field would sell me a "packet" containing an unknown quantity of seeds for 59¢. At Gurney's, twenty-five Sunspot seeds go for $1.30; fifty seeds would be $1.90 at Park's, $1.95 at Burpee; making Henry Field apparently the cheapest. To increase the confusion, some companies (Johnny's, Cook's Garden) deal in grams, others (R. H. Shumway's) in ounces and pounds; still others deal in the row length that a given quantity of seeds will presumably fill.

If you're ordering plants and things like onion sets or asparagus roots, as well as seeds, shipping charges can be steep; a good reason to order from companies close to home. But not *too* close to home or you'll have to pay state sales tax.

Then there are all the giveaways to cloud the issue; if I order $20 worth of merchandise by February 15, I'll be entitled to a free package of radish seed. If I spend $40 or more, they'll toss in a bunch of asparagus roots. I ought to know better, but I'm a sucker for bonuses. The phrase "Free gift!" never fails to excite me, despite its redundancy. Once the gift took the form of a dozen "hardy" gladiolus; forgetting that I don't like glads, I sent for them. I went to the trouble of planting them and in due time they came up, or rather sideways, the stems almost horizontal. They were salmon-orange and clashed horribly with the rest of the garden. Happily they didn't survive the following winter. Conclusion: There are no hardy gladiolus, and there is no free gift.

So you give up on choosing by cost—after all, seeds are cheap, you tell yourself—and decide to go for quality. Are there qualitative differences among the various purveyors? I've had good and bad experiences, none of them really conclusive. A bad experience was when a packet of what was supposed to be a tomato called Yellow Pear, bought from Pinetree Garden Seeds, turned out to be some nameless, worthless variety. The seller apologized and refunded the money. Of course, they couldn't replace the hours I spent raising those good-for-nothing plants,

". . . the thermometer outside my door reads eighteen below zero. I now know that spring will never come. I shall spend the rest of my life reading seed and plant catalogues . . ."

Jamaica Kincaid, in
The New Yorker,
March 29, 1993

or the cost of the potting soil, fertilizers, stakes, etc. It was an honest mistake, I guess. (I do appreciate Pinetree's policy of selling seeds in small, home gardener-scale quantities, and their low prices, so I continue to do business with them, warily.)

I've had so many bad experiences ordering plants by mail that I scarcely do it anymore. In many cases the plants themselves were not so much to blame as the circumstances of their arrival: too early to be planted, or too late, or not at all, or the one week that I wasn't there to accept them and the UPS man left them on the porch, where they froze/cooked/succumbed to fungus/withered. I can't deal with any more tragedies like these, so when I need to buy plants I go to a local garden center. The exception to this rule is roses, where the mail-order companies do seem to have better stock.

Finally, with time passing and every newspaper I read advising me to "order spring seeds now"; and then, "it's not too late to place your spring order"; or, worse: "it's time to start planting leek seeds," I make a rough list of plants I absolutely have to grow this year, and then begin looking for them. And right away things get complicated.

The Orange Pixie tomato that Burpee gave me as a free sample last year, and that everybody loved (it was cute-looking, early, trouble-free and delicious) isn't available this year! How can they do this to me? It's fortunate that I have so many catalogs: I finally track it down in the Tomato Grower's Supply Company catalog, thirty seeds for $1.45. As I fill out the order form, I note that if I order $7 or more I'll qualify for a free packet of Great White: "an heirloom variety that produces large white beefsteaks with an incredibly good, sweet flavor." That's a must-have. I quickly reach and pass the $7 limit. I'm cooking now.

But then my forward progress through the catalog order forms comes to a screeching halt. I've remembered something . . .

GHOSTS OF SEASONS PAST

I *have* some seeds, left over from last year or the year before or, I blush to admit, even earlier. They're in the pantry; in a rare moment of foresightedness I put them away in Ziploc bags.

Why do I have all this unused seed? I blame some of the excess on the catalog companies and their practice of packaging seed in quantities to suit *their* convenience, not mine. (Pinetree is one notable exception.) Pepper seed, for example, which is usually sold in packets of thirty to one hundred seeds. Imagine one hundred jalapeño pepper bushes, each one bearing hundreds of murderously hot little zingers! Not having a Mexican restaurant, I grow no more than a half-dozen pepper plants of any single variety, which leaves me with lots of partly used seed packets.

But in all honesty I must admit that most of these leftover seeds are the result of impulse buying. The kale that I ordered one year but didn't plant because by kale-planting time—July—I was no longer in planting mode. The radicchio that seemed like a good idea until I read the complex growing instructions on the package; instructions that were *not* included in the catalog copy. The snapdragon seed that was supposed to be started indoors in February but I got the flu and missed that boat.

Going through these grimy old seed packages is a chastening experience. As I inventory the old seeds, I swear to myself that this year I'll use or give away everything I buy.

My inventory will also have to include the seeds I've harvested myself, beginning with the Donnelly Tomatoes. Every year, for the last six, we've been growing these from seed we gathered the previous summer. It's named for my husband's son's ex-wife's father, who gave us the original seed. (Even nontraditional families have traditions.) The Donnellys are always successful, which is not true of all homegrown seeds. One year when I had a good zinnia crop I saved seeds from the prettiest flowers, carefully labeled as to color. The next year I planted them—there were hundreds—and exactly *one* came up.

The fact that I already have lots of seed, homegrown as well as leftovers, isn't going to stop me from buying more. No no no. The old stuff may be viable and it may not. Just in case those three packages of last year's morning glory seed are duds, I'll order a few this year. The possibility of facing a summer without morning glories is too awful to think about.

The inventory finally completed—mid-February!—I get back to work. Looking through all that leftover seed has, hopefully, taught me a lesson.

February Fever

My pencil races over the order forms. Cook's Garden has something called Cannelone Bean: can this finally be the large white Italian bean I encountered in a restaurant once and have always wanted to grow? At $2.10 for a two-ounce packet it's a bit steep, but I order it anyway. From the same company I choose a leek called Blue Solaise, unable to resist the copy: "This is the variety we grow for over-wintering here in Vermont, and we have dug them every month of the year. . . ." Yeah! I firmly resist the artichokes, though: last year my neighbors, Carol and Walter, tried to grow artichokes from seed and it was a disaster; the plants, seeded in March, planted outside in May, had not yet sent up a flower stalk when the hard frosts came in November. Rejecting the artichokes makes me feel really mature and sensible.

There are lots of other attractions in the Cook's catalog, but some of them can, I know, be found for less money elsewhere. I pick up the R. H. Shumway's catalog. I love this outfit for their straightforward slogan, *"Good seed cheap"*: you can't beat that. I also love the look of their catalog, and the wonderful old-timey black-and-white drawings they use. Their seeds certainly *seem* cheaper; a packet of Salad Bowl lettuce, enough to sow a fifty-foot row, costs only 90¢; for $2.85 I could get a whole ounce. Cook's Salad Bowl lettuce is $1.85 a two-gram packet, which sows a 75–100 foot row. I look it up: one ounce equals 28.3 grams, making Shumway's $2.85 packet a bargain, I think. You can't have too much Salad Bowl lettuce—unless, of course, you never get around to planting it all. I note that I have some Salad Bowl seed left over from last year; lettuce seed doesn't keep well at all, and after a year it's likely to have a very low germination rate. I erase the one-ounce packet of Salad Bowl from my Shumway order.

Maybe I'd do best to buy lots of small inexpensive packets of lettuce seed from Pinetree; that way I'd get more variety. Their seeds run 40¢ to 75¢ a packet for 150 seeds. (How long a row is 150 seeds? What is it in grams?) I choose Vulcan, Red Sails and Tom Thumb; then find Lollo Rossa and, a new one for me, Lingue de Canarino (canary tongue!) listed under Italian Vegetables; and Merveille de Quatre Saisons, in the Continental Vegetable section. Wouldn't it make better sense if Pinetree grouped all the lettuces together instead of segregating them by nationality?

Thoroughly confused by now, head throbbing, I pick up the Johnny's catalog, a favorite because they seem to have all the things I want and their instructions are so clear I often use the catalog as a reference book. Also, they understand indexing. Skipping past the hot peppers, which I'm not buying this year (the pantry is full of old unused seeds, the larder is bursting with dried and pickled peppers), I rapidly fill out the order form, picking Space spinach ("early," "easy to wash"), Blue Ballet squash (a winter squash that doesn't get out-of-bounds enormous), two tomato faves: Brandywine, a delicious and rather odd-looking heirloom, and Red Currant, which produces zillions of very tasty, pea-size fruit. Then I succumb to a new one: Johnny's 361. I've been looking for a beefsteak type that isn't too enormous, as I'm the chief tomato-eater in this family. It also claims to be early, compact, suited to the Northeast and resistant to some of the nasty diseases that afflict tomatoes (V,F2,N,T). It's a hybrid unlike the other two, which are heirlooms; placing me in the wishy-washy position of having a foot in both camps. Finally, I add two snap beans: Royalty Purple Pod, and a French filet type, Maxibel, as well as a tried-and-true fava bean called Loreta.

Setting Johnny's aside, I turn to Burpee's. If I order $10 worth of merchandise before February 28, Burpee's will send me a pair of "handy Garden Snips." (Here I go with the giveaways again!) I already have a pair of these little red-handled pruners, and I love them; they fit in a pocket and they cut just about anything. I take them everywhere I go. I'm in terror of losing the ones I have, and as they only ever seem to be available as bonuses I'm glad of a chance to get another pair. I pick out Sugar Snap peas, a winter squash called Lakota because it's so gorgeous, and lots of flowers: sweet peas, cosmos, snapdragons, sunflowers, marigolds. In no time I've achieved and passed the $10 limit. (See how they get me?)

Back to Shumway's for regular peas, Scarlet Runner beans, and more flowers: zinnias, morning glories, nasturtiums, more sunflowers, more cosmos. You cannot possibly have too many flowers. Or too many pumpkins: I choose a tiny one—Jack Be Little—and a giant, Big Max. Then back to Johnny's for the

I don't believe the half I hear,
Nor the quarter of what I see!
But I have one faith, sublime and true,
That nothing can shake or slay;
Each spring I firmly believe anew
All the seed catalogues say!

Carolyn Wells,
"One Firm Faith"

glamorous French Cinderella pumpkin, Rouge Vif D'Etamps. Then to the Thompson & Morgan "catalogue" (they're English, although they sell worldwide). This one is encyclopedic, with excellent color photos. They're expensive, but I always find they have some things, usually flowers, that I can't find anywhere else. (And if I stopped ordering from them they might stop sending that indispensable catalog.) From T & M I select blue and white salvias, white cosmos, schizanthus (delightful little orchid-like flowers), petunias . . . In no time I've gone over $20.

At Pinetree I fill up on herbs: four kinds of basil, dill, cilantro, fennel. Also arugula, mesclun and mache, to complete this year's salad pickings. I avoid beets, unhappily aware that I never got around to eating those I grew last year. But a miniature melon called Minnesota Midget captures my fancy; at 50¢ it's worth a try.

I pull out the calculator and start totaling: Pinetree, $17.20; Burpee, $19; Shumway, $23.10 . . . I've spent over a hundred dollars on seeds! And I haven't yet begun to study those pages with the really pricey—but essential—items: the plant foods and inoculants, the row covers, seedling flats, potting mixes, and all the other paraphernalia I'll need to get through spring and summer. I haven't yet ordered onion sets, or seed potatoes; haven't even *decided* whether I should give sweet potatoes a try this year. There are all the lilies and dahlias and other summer bulbs I'll want to fill out the perennial garden. I need roses, too . . .

And there are catalogs still untouched! Here's Seeds of Change, exclusively organic, totally open-pollinated, whose pages are as beautiful as their message is high-minded. And Shepherd's, with its eclectic, international selection of vegetables and flowers. And what about good old Gurney's, with its cheery, tabloid-like pages, and Park's, doggedly sending me catalog after catalog, week after week? Choosing a summer garden is as hard as choosing a college.

Finally, somehow, I finish filling out all the order forms and add up the appalling totals. I notice in passing that including the tomato seed saved from last year, I'll have *thirteen* separate varieties to grow in this summer's garden. I've done it again; I've set myself up for a summer of more work than I can do, more vegetables than I can eat, more flowers than I can pick. The number of actual holes I'll have to dig in the next few months must be literally astronomic. And a year from now, I know, I'll be looking at Ziploc bags full of leftover seed, wondering if they're still viable.

But it's too late to redo my order—and if I start crossing things out I might miss out on something really wonderful. I lick the envelopes and send them off. Peace descends on my household. I throw away the unused catalogs, clear the decks, and wait for the UPS man.

AFTERWORD

The more I garden, the less I know about it.

Gardening is infinitely complex. There are all kinds of rules, more than you can possibly learn in a lifetime; some of them are reasonable and some of them are nuts. Some are made to be broken and some can be broken only at peril.

Every day's mail brings new wisdom. Some of the most dearly held tenets turn out to be utterly false. Only the other day I learned from Allen Lacy's quarterly newsletter, *Homeground,* that the "ancient wisdom that holds it essential to put twenty-five-cent plants in fifty-cent holes" may be wrong. It seems it's just as good to put them into a hole only a bit bigger than the pot, water them well, and then cover them with a few inches of mulch. No more double digging! This is good news, well worth the $38 annual subscription price, even if I did read it twenty years ago in a book by Ruth Stout. Maybe next week it'll turn out that I don't have to dig eight-inch holes—in hard clay—to plant daffodil bulbs, they'll do as well or better under a light blanket of straw!

I'm reminded of the time I studied Italian. At first it seemed so lucid, so logical, after French (not to mention English); a language with a clear structure, easy-to-remember rules, consistent pronunciation. But then I came to a point where there were fewer rules and more and more exceptions; and then I went to Italy, where the natives of Lucca didn't sound remotely like those of Siena, and where day by day I felt that I knew less instead of more, to the extent that I could barely order my evening spaghetti.

Gardening, like learning Italian, is a humbling experience. Humbling experiences may have their uses, but unless you're a masochist they're not much fun. Why do it if it hurts?

Not because it makes us better persons. Gardening leads to jealousy, pride, greed, dishonesty and stealing. Who among us has not envied to the point of hatred the neighbor whose tomatoes ripen a week earlier than ours? Who hasn't found occasion to pinch a flower or a seedling from a public garden, or smuggle from abroad some contraband plant material?

Horticulture certainly doesn't make us healthier. Gardeners are said to be long-lived: or is it just that they *look* older, with their bent backs, gnarled hands and weathered, wrinkled skin? It's no coincidence that gardening magazines are full of advertisements for arthritis remedies.

Those rare moments of serenity—when the birds are chirping and the sun is shining and one's hands are happily plunged into the nice warm muck—are trifling compared with the hours of frustration and worry when the muck yields a crop of disappointment. But we do it, and we even enjoy doing it.

We garden because it is absorbing. It's like an endless soap opera. *All My Perennials,* perhaps; *One Row to Hoe; As the Worm Turns.* There's the perplexing mystery of who or what decimated the pumpkin patch; the near miraculous return from the dead of the dogwood; the sad fall from grace of the hybrid tea rose that reverted to some plebeian ancestor; the tragic tale of *Chaenomeles japonica,* nipped in the bud; the comic subplot of the cross-pollinating cucurbits. It's as engaging as life itself—but in the long run, not as terrible.

Writing this book, I've sometimes marveled that the various forces for chaos permit me to garden at all. How lucky I am that the opossum I saw on the back deck last March hasn't come back to raid my tomato plot; that the squirrel population mostly keeps to the trees. Even the rapacious Japanese beetles leave some berries on the bush. The drought could turn into one of the Plagues of Egypt, but hasn't. Last year's grievous winter dispatched roses, evergreens, fruit trees—but it miraculously spared the supposedly tender lavender.

Don't think I'm not grateful.

Sources and Suggested Reading

Abraham, Doc and Katy.
GROWING PLANTS FROM SEED.
New York: Lyons & Burford, 1991

THE AMERICAN GARDENER
(ed. Allen Lacy). New York:
Farrar, Straus & Giroux, 1988.

**THE AMERICAN HOME GARDEN
BOOK AND PLANT ENCYCLOPEDIA.**
Indianapolis: Curtis, 1963.

Austen, Jane.
MANSFIELD PARK.
New York: Penguin Classics,
1966.

Boland, Maureen and Bridget.
OLD WIVES' LORE FOR GARDENERS.
U.K.: Bodley Head, 1976.

A BOOK OF GARDENS
(ed. James Turner).
London: Cassell, 1963.

Brown, Jane.
VITA'S OTHER WORLD.
New York: Viking, 1985.

Church, Thomas.
GARDENS ARE FOR PEOPLE.
New York: McGraw-Hill, 1983.

Creasy, Rosalind.
COOKING FROM THE GARDEN.
San Francisco: Sierra Club Books,
1988.

Damrosch, Barbara.
THE GARDEN PRIMER.
New York: Workman, 1988.

Dworkin, Floss and Stan.
**FLOSS & STAN'S "WHY ARE MY
LEAVES TURNING YELLOW AND
FALLING OFF?" ANSWER BOOK.**
New York: Dutton, 1978.

*Enge, Torsten Olaf, and Carl
Friedrich Schröer.*
**GARDEN ARCHITECTURE IN
EUROPE: 1450–1800.**
Germany: Benedikt Taschen, 1990.

Fairbrother, Nan.
MEN AND GARDENS.
New York: Knopf, 1956.

THE GARDENER'S ESSENTIAL GERTRUDE JEKYLL
(ed. Elizabeth Laurence).
Boston: David R. Godine, 1986.

GARDENS OF EUROPE
(eds. Penelope Hobhouse and Patrick Taylor).
New York: Random House, 1990.

Girouard, Mark.
A COUNTRY HOUSE COMPANION.
New Haven: Yale University Press, 1987.

Goldbloom, Shelley.
GARDEN SMARTS: A BOUNTY OF TIPS FROM AMERICA'S BEST GARDENERS.
Old Saybrook, Conn.: Globe Pequot, 1991.

Hadfield, Miles.
THE ART OF THE GARDEN.
New York: Dutton, 1965.

————. **A HISTORY OF BRITISH GARDENING.**
U.K.: Penguin, 1960.

Hart, Rhonda Massingham.
BUGS, SLUGS & OTHER THUGS.
Pownal, Vt.: Storey Communications, 1991.

Henderson, Peter.
GARDENING FOR PROFIT.
New York: Orange Judd, 1874.

Hobhouse, Penelope.
GARDENING THROUGH THE AGES.
New York: Simon & Schuster, 1992.

JOHN CONSTABLE'S CORRESPONDENCE
(ed. R. B. Beckett).
U.K.: Suffolk Records Society, 1962.

Johnson, Hugh.
THE PRINCIPLES OF GARDENING.
New York: Simon & Schuster (Fireside Books), 1979.

Lacy, Allen.
GARDENING WITH GROUNDCOVERS AND VINES.
New York: HarperCollins, 1993.

————. **HOME GROUND: A GARDENER'S MISCELLANY.**
Boston: Houghton Mifflin, 1992.

Lloyd, Christopher.
THE WELL-TEMPERED GARDEN.
London: Penguin, 1978.

Mitchell, Henry.
THE ESSENTIAL EARTHMAN.
Bloomington: Indiana University Press, 1981.

Mitchell, Henry.
ONE MAN'S GARDEN.
Boston: Houghton Mifflin, 1992.

Mitford, Nancy.
THE SUN KING.
New York: Harper & Row, 1966.

Nichols, Beverley.
DOWN THE GARDEN PATH.
London: Antique Collector's
Club, 1982.

**THE OXFORD BOOK OF GARDEN
VERSE**
(ed. John D. Hunt).
New York: Oxford University
Press, 1993.

Page, Russell.
THE EDUCATION OF A GARDENER.
New York: Atheneum, 1962.

Perenyi, Eleanor.
GREEN THOUGHTS.
New York: Random House,
1981.

Pollan, Michael.
SECOND NATURE.
New York: Atlantic Monthly
Press, 1991.

**RODALE'S ALL-NEW ENCYCLOPEDIA
OF ORGANIC GARDENING.**
Emmaus, Pa.: Rodale, 1992.

**RODALE'S GARDEN INSECT, DISEASE
& WEED IDENTIFICATION GUIDE**
*(eds. Miranda Smith and Anna
Carr).*
Emmaus, Pa.: Rodale, 1988.

Reveal, James T.
GENTLE CONQUEST.
Washington, D.C.: Starwood,
1992.

Stein, Sara.
NOAH'S GARDEN.
Boston: Houghton Mifflin, 1993.

Stewart, Martha.
MARTHA STEWART'S GARDENING.
New York: C. N. Potter, 1991.

Stout, Ruth.
**HOW TO HAVE A GREEN THUMB
WITHOUT AN ACHING BACK.**
New York: Cornerstone Library,
1973.

Swain, Roger B.
THE PRACTICAL GARDENER.
Boston: Little, Brown, 1989.

Symes, Michael.
A GLOSSARY OF GARDEN HISTORY.
U.K.: Shire Garden History
Series, 1993.

Tompkins, Peter, and Christopher Bird.
THE SECRET LIFE OF PLANTS.
New York: Avon, 1973.

VAN GOGH: LETTERS FROM PROVENCE
(ed. Martin Bailey).
New York: Clarkson Potter, 1990.

White, Katharine S.
ONWARD AND UPWARD IN THE GARDEN (1959).
Farrar Straus Giroux, 1979.

Wilkinson, Albert E., and Victor A. Tiedjens.
THE HANDY BOOK OF GARDENING.
New York: Signet, 1950.

THE WISE GARDEN ENCYCLOPEDIA.
New York: HarperCollins, 1990.

About the Author

Abby Adams is a writer and gardener who lives in a 160-year-old farmhouse in upstate New York (zone 5) with her husband, author Donald E. Westlake. Together they garden some ten and a half acres, growing—with mixed success—a variety of vegetables and ornamentals.

Ms. Adams is the author of *An Uncommon Scold* (1,000 quotes from women) and, with her husband, *High Jinx* and *Transylvania Station*. Born and raised in New York City, she has at various times lived in San Francisco, in London, in Woodstock, New York, and on Fire Island. She has always gardened.